D0364038

Small is
Bountiful

Small is
Bountiful

Grow your own vegetables and fruit in small spaces

Liz Dobbs

Reader's
Digest

Published by The Reader's Digest Association, Inc.
LONDON • NEW YORK • SYDNEY • MONTREAL

Contributors

FOR TOUCAN BOOKS
Project Designer Mark Scribbins
Project Editor Theresa Bebbington
Managing Editor Ellen Dupont
Proofreader Caroline Hunt
Indexer Marie Lorimer
Photo Researcher Sharon Southren

FOR VIVAT DIRECT
Editorial Director Julian Browne
Art Editor Anne-Marie Bulat
Managing Editor Nina Hathway
Trade Books Editor Penny Craig
Picture Resource Manager Sarah Stewart-Richardson
Prepress Technical Manager Dean Russell
Production Controller Jan Bucil

NOTE TO OUR READERS
This publication contains the opinions and ideas of its author and is designed to
provide useful information to the reader. It is not intended as a substitute for the
advice of an expert on the subject matter covered. Products or active ingredients,
treatments and the names of organisations that appear in this publication are included
for informational purposes only; the inclusion of commercial products in the book
does not imply endorsement by Reader's Digest, nor does the omission of any
product or active ingredient or treatment advice indicate disapproval by Reader's
Digest. When using any commercial product, readers should read and follow all packet
instructions carefully.

The author and publisher specifically disclaim any responsibility for any liability,
loss or risk (personal, financial or otherwise) that may be claimed or incurred as a
consequence – directly or indirectly – of the use and/or application of any of the
contents of this publication.

Small is Bountiful is published in 2012 in the United
Kingdom by Vivat Direct Limited (t/a Reader's Digest),
157 Edgware Road, London W2 2HR
by arrangement with Toucan Books Ltd

Copyright © 2012 Toucan Books Ltd.

Reader's Digest is a trademark owned and under
licence from The Reader's Digest Association, Inc. and is
registered with the United States Patent and Trademark
Office and in other countries throughout the world.
All rights reserved.

All rights reserved. No part of this book may be
reproduced, stored in a retrieval system, or transmitted
in any form or by any means, electronic, electrostatic,
magnetic tape, mechanical, photocopying, recording
or otherwise, without permission in writing from the
publishers.

We are committed both to the quality of our products
and the service we provide our customers. We value your
comments, so please do contact us on **0871 351 1000** or
visit our website at **www.readersdigest.co.uk**

If you have any comments or suggestions about the
content of our books, email us at
gbeditorial@readersdigest.co.uk

ISBN 978 1 78020 065 1
Book Code 410-920-UP0000-1

Waltham Forest Libraries	
904 000 00264966	
Askews & Holts	17-May-2013
635.04 DOB	£14.99
3883670	⌐

Contents

Introduction

No garden? No problem! All you need are a few suitable containers and the right plants. You can grow some of your own food, even if you only have a small outdoor space without any garden soil.

Planting some attractive vegetable plants close to your home and growing them with ornamental flowers can be both practical and beautiful. You'll love picking fresh herbs every day from just outside the kitchen door – they will be so easy to reach when cooking. You can move the containers around, showing them off at their prime and moving them to a less conspicuous spot when they are at their least attractive. It will also be easier to move them away from nibbling creatures or to bring them inside if it gets too cold outside.

Even if you have a large garden, you may still want to grow vegetables in containers if most of your space is too shady. On the other hand, if your outdoor space is limited to just a balcony, patio or even a roof garden, growing vegetables in containers is often the only option available. However, there are more choices than you might have considered, such as using vertical spaces for pouches of fresh herbs.

This book aims to offer both inspiration and practical advice, showcasing the best plants to grow in a wide range of containers, from hanging baskets to large tubs. There are 34 projects that look as good as they taste, and detailed growing advice for more than 40 different vegetables, herbs and edible flowers. Even if you have never grown anything before, planting a few herbs or salad greens

A planting combining a rosemary with French marigolds complement the purple flowers in the bed. It would be just as attractive on its own near a kitchen door.

A mixed planting includes French tarragon and begonias, with frilly-leaved red lettuce making attractive edging plants.

Chemical-free living

If you can, it is best to avoid fungicides or pesticides. The majority of the plants grown for this book were planted in peat-free compost and raised without chemical sprays.

into three groups. Small Bites covers the fast crops such as salad leaves and herbs. These will grow in smaller pots or in planting arrangements that look pretty enough to sit on the patio, yet still yield plenty of edibles. Next, Bigger Servings looks at increasing the harvest by growing plants in larger containers. Last but not least, the focus on Going UP! is to make the most of vertical space to grow crops, whether it be window boxes of chillies, walls of flowering green beans or hanging baskets full of tomatoes.

Why not try some bowls of Speedy Stir-Fry on a patio table, a container of strawberries on a wall ledge or a tub of potatoes. The recipes will provide plenty of inspiration – no matter what your space. All the details are there for you to re-create the plantings

in containers is a wonderful place to start, and you will be able to enjoy and eat the results within one season. Even gardeners who are familiar with combining flowers and foliage in containers for ornamental displays will find some fresh ideas for being creative with edible plants.

with confidence or use them as a starting point for your own ideas. Some plants, such as herbs, tomatoes and courgettes, are so prolific that you will probably have more than you can eat. To help you use up your bounty, there are recipes with the relevant plantings.

Violas add a cheerful splash in a sea of green lettuce. However, there's another reason to grow these annuals – the petals are also edible.

The plantings

The projects have been developed around 'recipes', where we've put together plantings based on how you would use the harvest in the kitchen, whether it is a Taste of Italy, which provides tomato with basil to make bruschetta, or to have a mixture of mint available to pick. These planting recipes have been divided

Big Ideas for Small Spaces

One of the challenges of growing plants in a small space is to get as much as possible from them. When you plant a container with edible plants, also consider how to add something extra. Could you, for example, add some annual flowers or herbs for colour and also to attract beneficial insects? Or could you squeeze in another quick-growing plant such as lettuce or spinach before or after the main plantings? Here's a selection of our favourite ideas for getting the most out of small spaces, grouped by container size and location.

Small Bites

If you already plant a few flowerpots each spring with annuals to add summer colour to an outdoor space, all you need to do is adapt them. However, even if you don't have flowerpots, you can soon be planting your own fresh edibles.

The flowerpots and planters normally used for annuals are also suitable for producing a selection of tasty edibles. For example, in smaller containers under 40 cm (16 in) in diameter, you can grow a plentiful supply of tomatoes or chillies. At the least, you can have a daily supply of salad leaves, handfuls of fresh herbs, stir-fry greens and edible flowers for garnishes and herbal teas.

Apart from buying edible plants alongside your ornamentals, you won't need to invest in much more. The essentials are compost, slug control and watering equipment – which is just the same as for flowers. You will also need to purchase a balanced all-purpose fertiliser and a tomato fertiliser to increase your harvest.

Plant selection

For the biggest yield, grow vegetables in their own containers so there is less competition from other plants. However, choose plants that are ornamental such as chard, chillies or mixed lettuces. Alternatively, place ornamentals in other flowerpots alongside your vegetables. For example, use three glazed terracotta pots, each slightly smaller than the other. Plant a vegetable crop such as beans in the largest one, a salad leaf or herb in the middle one and an ornamental in the smallest one, then arrange them to make an attractive display. Make sure the larger plant doesn't cast a shadow on a smaller plant. If you have little space, you can grow vegetables and ornamentals together in one container, but you will have to compromise on your plant selection. Mixed herbs and edible flowers in the same container will work well because you will be picking smaller quantities.

Some modern varieties of vegetables, salad leaves and herbs are a better choice for container growing because they are more compact or colourful, or they mature faster, than older types. Tomato plants, for example, were originally straggling vines, but there are now varieties available in a wide range of habits, or shapes, from cascades for hanging baskets to squat bushes. Even a single chilli plant sitting on your table could give you more than

Colourful chard (above) makes an attractive display. Try planting them in a mixture of different containers and grouping them together.

A single planting of chillies (right) can supply enough peppers for the whole family – and also creates a festive focal point.

enough peppers and there are few prettier plants. Basil is a herb that has a lot of breeding work, and there are now selections in a range of leaf sizes and colours – not to mention some attractive flowering ones. Quick-maturing vegetable varieties from loose-leaf lettuce to Oriental greens to the humble radish mean that you can be serving fresh food from seeds within five weeks – even small spaces can be productive.

A room outdoors

If you have a sitting or entertaining area outside, chances are it is in a warm, sheltered spot near the house or at least within easy access. Most edibles will crop much better in a sunny, sheltered

A mixture of leaf shapes and textures adds interest to this grouping of vegetables and herbs, which includes chard, sage and basil, along with flowering nasturtiums.

position than in a dark corner or in a cold, windy place. For the best results, it makes sense to place containers on the patio. As an added bonus, you will find it easier to remember to provide them with the daily attention they need and to notice when they are ready for picking.

Off the ground

Outdoor features, from tabletops to benches, are suitable positions for small containers, which will keep them away from slugs and snails. Sow shallow bowls with mixed lettuces or Oriental greens, and they will crop in about five weeks. Several herbs such as prostrate rosemary, variegated sage and thyme also do well in shallow bowls. Sit them on a matching drip tray to keep the tabletop clean, but don't let their roots sit in water. Benches are useful places for hardening off young plants early in the season, because you can drape garden fleece over them. Low, wide walls are handy for potatoes growing in bags, carrots in flowerpots or window-box planters filled with salad leaves, herbs and bush tomatoes. The top of storage units – for example, for bicycles or firewood – are ideal for planters of mixed herbs.

Beds and borders

Most beds and borders have space either at the front or gaps between plants, usually at the start of the season or towards the

Arrange a grouping of containers with a selection of herbs such as thyme, basil and chives, along with different types of lettuces.

end, when plants have been cut back. Beds mulched with gravel can be a handy temporary home for pots of hardy herbs in late spring to early summer. In early autumn, once the front plants have been cut back, a row of flowerpots with chillies, parsley or thyme, for example, will add colour. An obelisk with climbing beans and nasturtiums weaving through it adds both colour and crops. Where the soil is bare, you can put down a paving slab to support the container. Remember to water and feed the plants, and protect them from slugs and snails.

Back doors and hidden corners

You can use locations that are not normally on display – for example, outside the kitchen door, passageways or under a tree – for growing food, but you should be realistic. Although a collection of herb plants outside the kitchen door might be handy for picking, if it is a cold, damp and shady spot, the plants will not thrive. In a shaded area try some woodland herbs in flowerpots, such as mint or parsley, or salad leaves. At least growing vegetables and herbs in small containers means you can move them into a sunny space every now and then. Potatoes in a large tub is an option for a partially shaded spot.

When choosing 'found' planters, make sure their size is suitable for the plants, such as this deep bread box for short carrot varieties.

Grow for it!

Ornamentals for a colour boost

- These flowers need sun but can cope with a dryish compost: marguerite daisy, gazania, pelargonium, petunia and zinnia.
- Flowers that tolerate partial shade and moist compost include alyssum, begonia, lobelia, impatiens, small fuchsias and French marigold.
- Two attractive foliage fillers are coleus and heuchera. Also look for variegated versions of culinary herbs and pelargonium to provide extra colour.

Out the front

If your front garden gets more sun than the back garden, why not use that space? You might want privacy, but your tomatoes will not mind passersby. Because you will be going in and out of the front door each day, you will be prompted to care for the plants. If you have a balcony, it could also provide enough extra shelter to make a difference in giving the plants an early start. Look for containers and plants that complement your building's style. They don't necessarily have to be bold – understated containers and plantings of herbs, vegetables and annuals may be more suitable to your surroundings and tastes than bright, colourful ones.

Bigger Servings

An increase in container size will considerably broaden your growing horizons, letting you grow a complete complement of vegetables and herbs with enough to preserve and store.

Increasing the size of a container to a minimum of 45 cm (18 in) in diameter will provide enough space for growing more than one type of edible plant. A larger container will also hold more volume, so you can grow root crops such as potatoes, carrots and beetroot, to a more mature size for storage. Vines and climbers, from courgettes and cucumbers to tomatoes and climbing beans, will be more manageable when it comes to watering and support, and often even only a couple of these plants will be enough to supply a family all summer. Although you can grow salad leaves and herbs in smaller flowerpots, they are much more productive in larger containers; in fact, you can be self-sufficient in salad leaves and have enough herbs to harvest and preserve for a winter supply.

Because there is a larger volume-to-surface-area ratio, the compost will be less susceptible to the extremes of waterlogging and drying out, and there is less risk of the roots getting too hot in summer. There will also be less day-to-day care required when growing vegetables in larger containers.

Productive or pretty?

Before acquiring the materials you will need and setting up the plantings, plan ahead. Is your priority to get a large harvest of potatoes or tomatoes? In that case, these container plantings will not be as attractive as a mixture of edible flowers or herbs, although a cook will be able to do more with a tub or two of potatoes or tomatoes than flowers. You can fit potato plants in woven, sturdy plastic bags or tubs among more ornamental containers. A good tip is to grow them in black containers at the back because they will be less noticeable than white or bright, colourful ones. Or you can move containers to a less prominent position; this is handy with larger tomato plants that start to look scraggly just when they have the most tomatoes on them.

Square-shaped containers provide more room for mixed plantings (left) such as these herbs. This attractive planter draws the eyes away from the plain pots used behind it for the taller vegetables.

Plain, deep pots and bags have been hidden by placing them inside more attractive, square wicker covers (right).

Round flowerpots and recycled materials

Large, conventional clay flowerpots can be expensive, so be prepared to think laterally. For example, plastic planters or recycled containers such as wooden apple crates, olive oil cans or old preserving pots can be suitable. If using wooden crates, first line them with plastic (make slits for drainage holes). Or use them to hold a group of pots of vegetables or herbs. Plastic buckets and laundry baskets are inexpensive, light and easy to move around. Laundry baskets, lined with plastic, will hold a few courgette plants, but add some nasturtiums or marigolds for colour. Don't take chances with your health by growing your edibles in recycled containers that once held chemicals – use only containers previously used for food or safe household situations.

Always position large pots and containers in their final location before filling them with compost. For potato or strawberry tubs, ones with handles are useful if you need to move them to protect from frost or birds. A plant trolley, wheelbarrow or even a skateboard will help move heavy pots, or consider attaching castors to wooden or plastic containers.

A metal planter with a mixture of both red and green pak choi, climbing beans and a feathery bronze fennel makes an attractive feature, replacing a bed in a very small space.

Linear planters

Large, square or rectangular planters make better use of space near buildings or features defined by straight lines and corners than round flowerpots. They suit a courtyard, patio, decking, porch, veranda, balcony or roof garden. A pair of square planters, one on each side of an entrance or at the top of steps, for example,

Manger-style planters make good use of space in a small garden. Put plants that need greater root depth in the centre.

could be formal with a standard bay tree clipped into shape and underplanted with neat thyme. They are useful for growing a short row of crops, and a line of planters alongside a sunny garage wall with trellis supports can supply you with a crop of climbing beans, with lettuces or spinach tucked in between. They are also useful for strawberries, because you can get more plants in them than in pots and baskets, and they are easier to cover with netting to protect them from birds. On a balcony or roof garden, plastic and fibreglass planters come into their own, often doubling up as screens to provide privacy.

Special planters are available for growing a large quantity of tomatoes, peppers or cucumbers in a small space with the minimum of mess. These self-contained systems have a built-in water reservoir – so there is no leaking on to a decking, for example – and there are attached supports for the plants. The container has wheels so the whole thing can be moved out of the way.

Containers that have wheels such as this Earthbox are useful for moving large plantings safely around your outdoor space.

Size with style

In a small garden where the containers are always visible, you can invest in one or two large elegant ones and fill them with a mixture of vegetables or herbs to make a feature of them. They are almost a substitute for a border or bed, and you can make them more so by planting some herbs at the bottom corners to anchor in the planting. For a mixture of vegetables and herbs, start with a tall or architectural subject – such as sweetcorn or a pepper – then plant some smaller subjects such as lettuce or parsley. Finally, add a bit of colour or a trailing plant, like a flowering herb such as chives or basil, or a colourful annual. Make sure you have a few extra plants waiting in the wings to fill the space after harvesting the main crop.

Raised beds

After a certain point, a particularly large planter might as well be a raised bed. There is no precise measurement that can signal when to switch from containers to a raised bed, but consider a raised bed when it gets too expensive to buy enough containers, or when they are too heavy or cumbersome to move. A raised bed is usually, but not always, in contact with the ground beneath, forming four sides for holding topsoil and well-rotted organic compost. Raised bed kits are available in plastic, metal or wood. Most are modular and come with accessories such as hoops for supporting crop covers. You can also make your own from sawn wood.

Potato plants provide plenty of green foliage but few flowers, so place them where they won't need to be the centre of attention.

Grow for it!

Flowers for after the harvest

- After potatoes have been harvested, the leftover compost can be reused; for example, it is perfect for planting tulip bulbs in autumn. When spring arrives, add lettuces and tarragon; then remove the tulips after flowering and replace with bedding plants around the lettuces and tarragon.
- Ornamental perennials, such as agapanthus, day lilies, fuchsia, stonecrop or dwarf rudbeckia, can replace crops harvested in early to midsummer. Plant the perennials in the centre and plant low-growing herbs around the edge for a late display.

Going UP!

By simply adding a basket of tomato plants hanging from your balcony, you are practising 'vertical' gardening. Look up and around to see what other growing spaces you have – perhaps a sunny wall or fence – then select containers for planting.

Traditional containers such as hanging baskets, wall planters and window boxes are ideal for tomatoes, chillies, dwarf beans and lettuces, as well as herbs and edible flowers. Some containers have extra features to make vertical gardening easier, such as planters that fit over the tops of railings, baskets with built-in water reservoirs and window boxes that come with inner liners so you can easily swap a tired harvested planting for fresh new plants. If you position planters above head height, you will need to make sure they are well secured with brackets of the appropriate size and strength.

Climbing success

Attractive and bountiful climbing bean plants make excellent use of vertical space. The plants can grow in the ground or in a large

Grow runner beans up a pergola (left) for a summer screen, colourful flowers, and supply of beans.

These rustic-looking window boxes (opposite) have liners inside them, so the display can be changed during the season.

flowerpot or tub. For support, use either a temporary wigwam of bamboo poles or grow the plants against a permanent structure such as a trellis, fence or pergola, mixing them in with ornamental annual climbers such as morning glories.

Wall space

You can attach new innovations such as flexible planting pouches or pockets to walls to 'green' them. The most advanced ones are modular systems with a built-in automatic-drip irrigation system that can be assembled to create something to fit within your space. These planters take up little room and create exciting opportunities for growing food in a courtyard or a balcony. An

 Grow for it!

Plants for high places

- For sunny surfaces where watering can be difficult, choose plants that can tolerate dry conditions; these include herbs such as thyme, sage, dwarf lavender, oregano and a small rosemary.
- Sun with a moist compost provides the ideal conditions for strawberries, bush or tumbling tomatoes, or a crop of dwarf beans or bush peas.
- For partial shade with a moist compost, choose parsley, chives, loose-leaf lettuce varieties and rocket. To make a really pretty display, you can add violas.

expanse of plants on vertical surfaces, particularly in urban areas, cools the interior and surroundings in summer.

On a practical note, hanging baskets work well where ground space is limited. However, you also need to be sure their containers do not protrude along walkways. Wind is a challenge for the plants, and you will see them wilt if the roots cannot supply the leaves with

enough water to replace the moisture lost by wind. Make sure the plants have grown enough so their roots are holding the compost together before arranging them, and harden off plants well (see page 107) before putting them into their final positions. Finally, make sure the plants will have a sufficient water supply.

Hanging baskets and wall planters

For your first baskets, or if you have little time, try the more modern designs of wicker or coir lined with plastic; you just need to position the plants at the top, unlike other types in which they are inserted in the sides. Include one or two trailing plants, even if these are not edible, to soften the display. There are now hybrid containers that are a cross between a basket and a plant pouch. They can be awkward to plant, but they look attractive once the plants have covered the container, and they usually have a water reservoir. Wall planters are more ornamental than productive, but a group of three glazed pots arranged on a wall can supply some fresh herbs. Use small drought-tolerant herbs, such as thyme, dwarf lavender and chives, plus a garlic or even a bush chilli.

Not much will grow under a mature shady tree, but it does provide a spot to hang a basket of loose-leaf lettuces, which prefer protection from the sun during the summer.

 Grow for it!

Trailing flowers

- Edible plants that trail include tumbler-type tomatoes, trailing nasturtiums and trailing violas.
- There is a wider range of non-edible annuals with flowers that last all summer; choose from *Bacopa cordata*, *Sanvitalia procumbens* and trailing varieties of begonia, bidens, calibrachoa, fuchsia, petunia and verbena.
- Trailing plants with bright foliage add colour, too; for example, *Dichondra* 'Silver Falls' and a silver-leaved helichrysum both provide silver foliage. A sweet potato vine offers ornamental foliage in 'Sweetheart Purple'.

Balconies and boundaries

Despite their name, window boxes can also be fitted to the sides of balconies. The ideal place is in a sunny spot that you can reach safely and near a water supply. Also remember the importance of secure fittings. Some containers are designed to straddle balconies, with the compost weighing them down in place. Drainage holes are vital, but after watering, the compost can be washed through and leave a mess. Line the container with newspaper; it will slowly disintegrate, but by then the compost will be held in place by the roots. Or use plastic containers with built-in reservoirs. Fencing or trellis screens can become productive by using plant pouches or hook-on wooden shelves. Or attach brackets for hanging baskets to fence posts.

Wide steps provide a setting for growing cucumbers with attractive yellow flowers. This variety forms round cucumbers.

Stages and steps

Display shelves with tiers can hold a number of small flowerpots, offering an array of herbs and salad leaves, as well as colour from chillies and tiny tomatoes. The simplest are wooden 'ladder' types ideal for outside a kitchen door. More stylish is a metal French etagere displaying ceramic flowerpots, taking centre stage on a patio. Filled with Mediterranean herbs plus a small citrus, geraniums or a miniature rose, a corner etagere will also make good use of space. Remember to put shade-tolerant parsley and lettuces on lower shelves or move the plants around. A wide flight of steps can be home to edibles, too, especially in a shady space where steps going up might be the only sunny spot. Be aware of tripping hazards and make sure the pots cannot be blown over by the wind.

Roof gardens

The increasing interest in edible gardening in cities has refreshed the idea of roof gardens with new lightweight materials. Opt for lightweight containers such as wood, plastic or fibreglass, and use a lightweight compost, or try hydroponic systems that rely on water rather than soil. You can also attach plant pouches to screens used for shelter and privacy.

Hanging baskets are a good choice for tumbling cherry tomatoes, keeping them off the ground away from the soil.

Small Bites

This selection of planting ideas is suitable for the smallest containers. Keeping the containers small makes them easy to move around – from outdoor tabletops to benches, from patio corners to border edges. And you can grow your own vegetables and herbs in even the tiniest spaces. Fast-growing leafy crops, such as salad leaves and herbs, and single specimens of prolific vegetables, such as chillies and certain types of tomatoes, suit small containers. Adding annual edible flowers, such as pot marigolds along with small bedding plants, will add colour to your vegetable haven.

Salad Bowl

This mixture of salad leaves, herbs and flowers yields a variety of edible treats from early summer to autumn, providing a constant supply of fresh lettuces, oregano and edible petals. The planting is portable – simply pick up the basket and move it to a new position. Keep the basket high up, on a table or elsewhere, away from slugs and snails that will be attracted to the lettuces.

You will need

Wire basket with handle,
  20 x 35 cm (8 x 14 in)

Lining material such as coir or
  sheet moss (dried sphagnum
  in sheets)

Sheet of plastic 20 x 30 cm
  (8 x 12 in)

Compost

2 lettuce plants

1 oregano plant

2 French marigold plants

Planting your pot

1. Line the basket with the lining material, letting it drape over the edge of the basket. Place a sheet of plastic along the base of the basket (to prevent too much water draining through), then add the compost. Trim the lining material to just below the edge of the basket a few days after planting up.

2. Plant the basket in spring using young plants. Lettuces and oregano (*Origanum vulgare*) are hardy, but French marigolds are tender, so keep the planting somewhere light and frost free until there is no danger of frost, then harden off and move outside.

3. Keep the compost moist, and in hot sunny weather move the basket to partial shade. You can harvest heart-forming lettuces whole, then remove the root and add new young lettuce plants. Or, if growing loose-leaf lettuces, use scissors to cut little and often.

4. Oregano leaves have the best flavour before the plant flowers, but the flowers are edible, too, and they are loved by butterflies and bees. If the plant starts to crowd out the lettuces, cut it back. Deadhead French marigolds often to keep more flowers forming.

 Grow for it!

New ways, old baskets

This container is a copy of a traditional French market basket, made of steel wire mesh with a wooden handle. Its practical design allows the vegetables to be harvested, then rinsed under running water while they are still in the basket. These strong baskets, if lined, also make lightweight, portable containers for salads and herbs. You can keep one on an outdoor table or bench, or hang it on a door handle. You may find models with wire lids that can be unclipped with pliers if you want to use them as containers.

Speedy Stir-fry

Stir-frying is one of the quickest ways to prepare tasty nutritious greens, and the ingredients are ultrafast growers, too. You can sow pak choi and other Oriental greens in the same container. A terracotta bowl, the type often used for small spring bulbs, is just about big enough to provide several servings. Here, a white-stemmed pak choi is teamed with red mustard leaf.

You will need

Shallow terracotta bowl, with a drainage hole, 30 cm (12 in) in diameter, 15 cm (6 in) deep

Drainage material such as crocks

Compost

Packet of mixed Oriental greens or separate packets of pak choi and red mustard leaf seeds

Balanced all-purpose fertiliser

Fine mesh cover

Planting your pot

1. Put just a few crocks over the drainage hole, then fill the bowl with compost, firm the surface and sow the seeds 2.5 cm (1 in) apart.

2. Thin out in stages by removing every other plant for baby leaves and leave about six pak choi plants to grow bigger for cooked greens. Prioritise the pak choi over the red mustard leaf, as the latter is very hot and not as useful in the kitchen.

3. Keep the compost continually moist so the pak choi grows without disturbance to its growth and produces succulent stems. Feed with a balanced all-purpose fertiliser every other week to keep the leaves healthy.

4. Pak choi attracts slugs and snails; keeping the bowls on outdoor tables will make it difficult for them to reach. Flea beetles can disfigure leaves; use a fine mesh cover if they are around.

5. Cut alternate pak choi plants off at the stem, leaving room for the others to grow. Snip mustard leaves off as required.

Oriental greens stir-fry

In a small mixing bowl, prepare a sauce by whisking together 3 tablespoons soya sauce, 1 tablespoon rice wine winegar, 1 tablespoon oyster sauce, 3 cloves finely chopped garlic, 1 teaspoon red chilli flakes, 1 teaspoon sugar and ½ teaspoon black ground pepper; set aside. Rinse and dry 6 heads pak choi; if large, cut in half lengthways. Then heat 1 tablespoon rapeseed oil in a wok or large heavy-based frying pan over a high heat, add the pak choi and stir-fry for 1 minute. Pour over the sauce, cover with a lid and cook over a medium heat for about 3 minutes until tender. Serve as a side dish.

Trio of Chillies

Aficionados of the chilli will focus on its shape, colour, flavour and hotness. When growing your own chillies, choose varieties that yield a crop before the end of the growing season in your area. The size of the plants varies – this trio represents the range of plant sizes and shapes you might come across, including a tall Spanish Padron pepper.

You will need

Wicker basket, 40 cm (16 in) in diameter, 30 cm (12 in) deep

Bushel basket, 25 cm (10 in) in diameter, 25 cm (10 in) deep

Wicker basket, 25 cm (10 in) in diameter, 20 cm (8 in) deep

Compost

1 Padron pepper

2 other chilli varieties in different sizes, one compact but high yielding, and another upright and early

6 small coriander plants

Tomato fertiliser

Planting your pots

1. Buy a plant of each variety instead of growing from seed. The plants are frost sensitive, so buy plants in small 10 cm (4 in) diameter pots and keep them in a light, frost-free place. Transfer them into larger pots, and then pinch out the growing tips to keep the plants bushy. Or you can wait until there is no more risk of frost and buy more mature specimens in 20 cm (8 in) diameter pots that have been already pinched out.

2. Place mature plants into slightly larger attractive flowerpots. Make sure you drill drainage holes, if necessary, so water doesn't sit in the base. Grow a compact, spreading plant in its own pot. Add coriander plants around an upright plant. The plants might need staking, depending on the variety and how much of the tips were pinched out earlier.

3. Feed the chilli plants with a tomato fertiliser when the first flowers start to appear, and supply water during dry spells. When watering spreading plants, direct the water at the compost, not the plant. Cut the leaves of the coriander plant, using scissors, as required.

Tapas peppers

Padron peppers, or Pimientos de Padrón, were brought to Spain by Mexican monks in the eighteenth century, where they are still grown and served up whole in tapas dishes.

Cut 8–10 green chillies from the plant, leaving the stalk intact. Wash and dry them. Sauté the whole chillies in hot olive oil in a frying pan over a high heat until the skin is blistered, turning occasionally with tongs. Sprinkle with salt and serve. Eat by holding the stalk. The green chillies are sweet but 1 out of 10 is hot, so be prepared for heat.

Mini Moussaka

Aubergines take a while to get going, but as the season progresses they become substantial patio plants with ornamental flowers, followed by colourful edible fruit. For this planting, a silver metal pot was used to house a single aubergine plant. Ornamental flowers are included to provide more visual interest through the summer, as well as herbs to use with the aubergines.

You will need

Galvanised metal pot, with drainage holes, 38 cm (15 in) in diameter, 33 cm (13 in) high

Compost

Drainage material such as crocks or gravel

1 aubergine plant

1 verbena plant (trailing type)

1 *Convolvulus sabatius* or 1 oregano plant

3 thyme plants

Tomato fertiliser

Planting your pot

1. Aubergines need a long, warm growing season to fruit, but they are also sensitive to cold. To grow one or two plants, wait until late spring, then buy young plants. Transfer them to larger pots a couple of times to avoid disturbing root growth and keep them in a bright, warm location. For a bushy plant, pinch out the growing tips when they are 20 cm (8 in) high.

2. In early summer they will be ready to be transferred to the final pot. Add drainage material to the base of the pot and then the compost; metal and lightweight pots need heavier drainage to help prevent the planting tipping over. Plant the aubergine in the centre, at the same level it was in its original pot. Make sure the plant is straight; it will probably need supporting stakes.

3. The space between the plant and the edge of this container is limited. We added two trailing ornamentals for their lavender blooms, but you could use oregano. Thyme fills in neatly around the edge. All these plants like warm, sunny sites and can tolerate dryness at the roots.

4. Water the aubergine well and give it a tomato fertiliser when the first flowers start to form. When they are ready for harvesting, cut off the fruit. Wear gloves if the aubergine variety has spines. Towards the end of the growing season, if the fruit is still developing, move the pot under cover at night.

Bright Lights

This no-nonsense planting is filled with edibles that are easy to grow from seed or young plants. Each crop is grown in its own pot for maximum yield. The trio offers both young pickings for salad and mature vegetables for cooking. Chard leaves are a spinach substitute, and the stems can be stir-fried. Carrots can be steamed, boiled or stir-fried, and lettuces can be made into soup.

You will need

1 glazed terracotta pot, with drainage holes, 30 cm (12 in) in diameter, 23 cm (9 in) deep

1 glazed terracotta pot, with drainage holes, 25 cm (10 in) in diameter, 12.5 cm (5 in) deep

1 glazed terracotta pot, with drainage holes, 23 cm (9 in) in diameter, 20 cm (8 in) deep

Drainage material such as crocks

Compost

Chard 'Bright Lights' seeds or young plants

Carrot seeds or seed tape

Lettuce seeds or young plants

Fine mesh cover

Balanced all-purpose fertiliser

Planting your pots

1. Fill each pot with drainage material and compost. Firm the surface so you can sow directly into the pots, then cover with a thin layer of compost. Alternatively, transplant young plants into the pots.

2. 'Bright Lights' is the best chard for containers, because the colourful mixture of stems are so ornamental, and they are also milder in taste than the red type. Sow seeds in modular trays and transplant them into their final pot once you can identify the colours you want – yellow, pink and orange are tasty. Use the biggest of the three pots; the roots will eventually fill it. Keep the compost moist to prevent the stems becoming tough.

3. Carrots need their own pot so the seeds can germinate without being disturbed; they also need less water than leafy crops. For long roots, choose deep containers such as buckets, but for baby or stubby carrots, a 20 cm (8 in) deep pot is fine. Scatter the seeds; later thin seedlings to 2.5 cm (1 in) apart. Lift the pot 90 cm (3 ft) off the ground or use a fine mesh to deter carrot fly.

4. Lettuce roots are shallow so use the smallest pot. In this example, a couple of loose-leaf lettuces have been left to fill the pot and will be harvested all at once. Provide a balanced all-purpose fertiliser, if needed. Keep the soil moist and move to a shaded spot in hot weather to keep the leaves sweet and tender.

Flowers for Salads

Here is a colourful mixture of edible flowers and foliage in a light container, ideal for the edge of a patio, top of a low wall or a table. The highlight is the mauve spires of African basil contrasting with the orange pompons of the pot marigold, but also waiting in the wings are edible mauve flowers to come from the oregano and chive plants. All the flowers will attract beneficial insects, too.

You will need

A fibreglass oval container, 40 cm (16 in) long, 20 cm (8 in) at its widest point and 18 cm (7 in) deep

Drainage material such as a few crocks or polystyrene packing peanuts

Compost

2 'African Blue' basil plants

2 pot marigolds (Calendula officinalis 'Porcupine')

1 young oregano plant

2 young chive plants

2 basil plants with colourful leaves, such as purple

2 cinnamon basil plants or other small-leaved basil plants

Planting your pot

1. Fill the container with some drainage material such as broken crocks or packing peanuts, then add the compost. Keep everything as lightweight as possible so the display can be moved around.

2. When planting an oval shape, start in the middle at the widest point – with the ornamental 'African Blue' basils and oregano plant, then work towards the edge. The 'Porcupine' pot marigold was chosen for its brightly coloured quilled petals and long flowering period, but any compact variety will do.

3. Fill in the gaps with smaller plants such as a selection of different basil plants and some young chive plants at each end; the latter will soon produce mauve pompon flowers. The container needs a warm, sunny site and minimal watering because all are drought tolerant.

4. Harvest flowers as required in the morning after the dew has dried. The chives and oregano can be cut back to the base if they get scruffy, and they will produce new leaves. Pot marigolds can get powdery mildew in hot or overcrowded conditions; remove affected leaves. Basil blackens and dies at the first sign of frost; when this happens, it's time to dismantle the planting.

Rally Round Rosemary

Left to its own devices, rosemary is a sprawling shrub, but here it has been trained into an edible topiary and planted in a good-quality flowerpot. The companion plants were chosen because they are neat and low-growing, so they will not distract from the shape. This planting makes an attractive front door display, and a pair on each side of an entrance would add a formal touch.

You will need

Frost-resistant terracotta flowerpot, 32 cm (13 in) in diameter, 30 cm (12 in) high

Drainage material such as crocks, gravel or polystyrene packing peanuts

Loam-based compost

Horticultural grit

1 rosemary plant, already trained as a standard

3 calibrachoa plants

1 variegated lemon thyme plant

Planting your pot

1. Despite the dainty appearance of the top growth, the rosemary's roots are surprisingly big and will take up most of a pot of this size. Add about 5 cm (2 in) of drainage material to the base of the pot, then plant the rosemary at the same level it was in its original pot, using a loam-based compost with some grit mixed in (about a handful to every four handfuls of compost). Make sure the plant is as straight as possible; if it is young, the plant might need the supporting stake left in place until the main stem stiffens.

2. For summer colour, plant the calibrachoa around the edge. These are neat-growing tender annuals with small petunia-like flowers that come in a range of colours, so you can match their colour to the flowerpot. You can divide a low-growing thyme and plant the divisions to fill in the gaps under the rosemary stem, but the planting would look equally attractive with a mulch of small grey gravel. Allow the compost to dry out slightly between watering.

3. The rosemary will flower in spring. After flowering, you can trim it to shape and use the trimmings in the kitchen. Cut back the thyme if it gets straggly.

4. The calibrachoa will die once the first frost arrives. Remove and replace it with purple violas or more grey gravel. The other plants are evergreen and will survive in most areas during the winter, especially in the shelter of an entrance.

Pick a Pepper

Sweet red peppers are useful in the kitchen, and they look good in the garden, too. In this case, a small variety has been partnered with a bowl-shaped outdoor container. The pot matches the low but spreading shape of the plant, and is the right shape for a tabletop or low wall. There is still room to squeeze in some young prostrate rosemary and pretty flowers for edging.

You will need

Glazed, bowl-shaped terracotta pot, 35 cm (14 in) in diameter, 18 cm (7 in) deep

Small square of mesh

Drainage material

Compost

1 small sweet red pepper plant

2 small prostrate rosemary plants

2 *Bacopa* species plants or any ornamental trailing plant that matches the container

Tomato fertiliser

Planting your pot

1. If the drainage hole is large and the pot will be on a table, cover the hole with a piece of mesh so the compost does not get washed through it, then add drainage material.

2. Half-fill the pot with compost, then tip the sweet pepper plant out of its pot and place it in the centre of the container.

3. Position the rosemary and *Bacopa* plants in gaps around the edge of the pot. Fill with the compost, making sure there is about 2.5 cm (1 in) between the top of the pot and the surface of the compost for the planting to be watered without the compost washing out. Firm the compost in gently. The planting cannot be placed outside until all danger of frost has passed because the sweet pepper is frost sensitive.

4. Supply water during dry spells. When watering the container, avoid soaking any sweet pepper fruit and foliage, because it can cause rotting. Give the sweet pepper a tomato fertiliser when the first flowers start to appear.

5. If foliage is covering the developing fruit, trim it off so the fruit can ripen in the sun. Slugs can eat the fruit, so keep the container off the ground and use copper tape around the outside edge of the container.

6. Cut the rosemary with scissors when needed; cut off the peppers when the skin is red.

Taste of Italy

The smooth line of this stylish container looks at home in a contemporary setting. Using a tomato plant and a circle of sweet basil, the planting is restrained but the ingredients for a tasty bruschetta are in place. The container looks like terrazzo – a combination of marble chips and concrete polished until smooth – but it is, in fact, lightweight fibreglass.

You will need

Fibreglass planter, with a terrazzo finish, 35 cm (14 in) in diameter, 45 cm (18 in) deep

Drainage material such as crocks or polystyrene packing peanuts

Compost

Support such as a garden cane or metal spiral support, plus garden twine

1 indeterminate trained tomato plant

6 sweet basil plants, or 3 sweet basil plants and 2 winter savory

Tomato fertiliser

Planting your pot

1. Add at least one-third drainage material, then compost to the container. Plant the tomato plant along with a support such as a garden cane or metal spiral support.

2. Plant the sweet basil plants around the tomato plant. Both plants are frost-sensitive, so wait until there is no danger of frost before hardening off and leaving them outside.

3. Water during dry spells. When watering the container, avoid soaking any sweet basil foliage. Give the tomato plant a tomato fertiliser when the first flowers start to appear. Remove side shoots from the tomato plant to train it upright, and pinch out the tips of the basil plants to encourage plenty of basil foliage. The tomato plant might need tying to the support with garden twine.

4. Harvest the basil leaves as required, and pick the tomatoes when almost ripe, before the skins split.

Bruschetta

Chop 4 tomatoes and put them into a bowl. Tear 4 basil leaves into pieces and add them to the bowl, then pour in 2 tablespoons of olive oil. Add ½ teaspoon salt and ground pepper to taste. Mix and let the flavours combine for a few minutes. Toast 8 slices of Italian bread lightly. Peel a garlic clove and cut it in half, then rub the toasted bread with the cut side. Discard the garlic. Place 2 slices of bread on each plate, and spoon on the tomatoes. Drizzle with a little olive oil and scatter 2 or 3 whole basil leaves over them to garnish.

Lemon Trio

Citrus plants do not have the monopoly on a refreshing lemon flavour. Here, three of the best – lemon verbena, lemon grass and lemon balm – are brought together using a nest of three ceramic flowerpots. White summer flowers have been added for early interest, since the lemon grass and lemon verbena will take a while to fill their pots.

You will need

A nest of three ceramic pots, 23, 30 and 40 cm (9, 12 and 16 in) in diameter

Drainage material such as crocks

Compost

1 lemon verbena *(Aloysia triphylla)*

3 lemon grass *(Cymbopogon citratus)*

1 variegated lemon balm *(Melissa officinalis)*

5 annual chrysanthemums or other daisy-flowered bedding plants such as marguerites

3 *Bacopa* species plants

Planting your pots

1. Line the base of the pot with crocks and fill with an ordinary compost, or use a loam-based compost to keep the plants going year after year.

2. A small leafy lemon verbena bought in spring will grow into a white flowering shrub by summer. In autumn, the leaves drop off. Keep the woody stems frost-free in a greenhouse until they sprout the following year. *Bacopa* are low-growing plants, so the lemon verbena's woody framework can develop. The flowers are too small to deadhead, so remove the *Bacopa* when past its best.

3. Lemon grass is a tender plant whose leaves and swollen stem bases are used in Asian dishes. Grow this tropical native as a summer patio plant. Put the lemon grass in the centre, then plant around with chrysanthemums.

4. Grow lemon balm on its own in the smallest pot. This perennial can be invasive, so growing it in a container is a good way to control it. An alternative plant for this pot size is a lemon-scented pelargonium, although it is not hardy.

5. Use some of the young leaves immediately, particularly the lemon verbena and lemon balm, because they have more flavour before flowering. At the end of the season, remove the chrysanthemums, then move the containers to a frost-free location if you want to keep the other plantings.

Mint Condition

Capture the refreshing aroma of fresh mint in the smallest of spaces by confining these spreading perennials in flowerpots. Each one of these three flowerpots has a mint with a slightly different flavour: classic spearmint, stronger peppermint and the milder apple mint or variegated pineapple mint. The pot should be at least 35 cm (14 in) in diameter, large enough to hold a small mint for a season.

You will need

3 thick terracotta pots,
  35 cm (14 in) in diameter,
  30 cm (12 in) high

Rich compost

1 peppermint (Mentha × piperita)

1 spearmint (Tashkent or
  Moroccan mint, M. spicata)

1 apple mint or pineapple
  mint (plain or variegated,
  M. suaveolens)

Planting your pots

1. Plant each mint in a container filled with a rich compost. Place the finished flowerpots in sun or partial shade; they will need watering regularly to keep a supply of fresh leaves.

2. Start to pick the leaves as soon as the plants are growing. First pinch out the growing tips for small quantities; later, shear the plant after flowering to stimulate new foliage. The plants flower in summer; these flowers are edible and also attract butterflies and bees.

3. Each year in autumn, replant the mint into a larger container with fresh compost, as once a plant reaches the edges of its container it starts to deteriorate. Mint can be vulnerable to diseases such as mildew and rust if starved or overcrowded; in such cases, dispose of all the plants and start again with fresh mint.

 Grow for it!

Make more of mint

Mint tea is said to be good for digestion and is often drunk at the end of a meal. Simply add a few sprigs of spearmint or peppermint to hot water and strain after 5 minutes.

The mints featured here are herbaceous perennials, so they will die down in autumn. You can keep some growing in a flowerpot on a kitchen windowsill during the winter, or you can harvest all of the mint, wash it, chop it up and freeze in ice-cube trays with a few drops of water.

Bigger Servings

By increasing the size of the container, the quantity and range of edible plants you can grow will increase, too. Just imagine being self-sufficient in salad leaves and courgettes in the summer, with enough beetroot to pickle and herbs to dry for the winter. Root, bulb and tuber crops from carrots, shallots and potatoes become a possibility when using a deeper container. You can also include some perennial treats such as roses (try making the rose syrup on page 50), or even create an impressive feature with home-grown lemons.

Flowers for Flavour

The sweet smell of roses, a waft of lavender and the delicate fragrance of pinks are the essence of summer. Here, together in one pot, are the most evocative. Capture some of their fragrance to use in your cooking by picking buds and petals for flavouring syrups and sugars. Choose a frost-resistant container if you want to keep these perennials going.

You will need

Frost-resistant ceramic container, 50 cm (20 in) in diameter, 30 cm (12 in) deep

Drainage material such as crocks

Loam-based compost

1 patio standard (tree-form) rose with pink or red scented blossoms*

3 English lavenders (Lavendula angustifolia)*

3 scented pinks (Dianthus)*

Rose fertiliser

*Buy organically raised plants, or take your own cuttings of lavender or pinks to grow into mature plants. Alternatively, check when the plants were last treated and with what, so you can allow for at least a couple of weeks before harvesting. Pink and red roses are the best for cooking.

Planting your pot

1. Preparation is the key if you are intending to keep the plants in the container for several years. Place the pot in its final position before planting. Add a generous layer of crocks to help water drain, then fill with a good-quality, loam-based compost.

2. Start with the rose, taking care to plant it at the same level it was in its original pot and to centre it as vertical as possible. Plant the lavenders and pinks alternately around the rose.

3. The rose will need to be kept moist, but the other plants will cope with drying out between watering. Feed with a rose fertiliser three or four weeks after planting.

4. Harvest the blooms in the morning once the dew has dried. Deadhead faded blooms to keep more flowers coming through the summer. You can use lavender foliage sparingly in cooking.

Rose syrup

For the best results, choose fragrant roses and pick them in the morning. To prepare the roses, shake to remove any insects, then rinse under a fine jet of water. Pull off the petals and place on kitchen paper. Using scissors, cut off the bitter white part at the base of each petal. In a saucepan over a medium heat, add 240 ml (8 fl oz) water, 600 g (1 lb 5 oz) sugar and 20 g (¾ oz) rose petals. Bring to the boil and cook for 10 minutes, or until thickened into syrup; do not allow to caramelise. Remove from the heat. Strain through muslin into a sterilised glass jar, leave to cool, then refrigerate for up to 2 weeks. Add the syrup to sparkling water or champagne, or pour over fruit or Madeira cake.

Outdoor Salad Bar

Making and growing your own salad bar will provide you with a steady supply of fresh salad leaves. Using three modular boxes makes it easier to sow seeds on a regular basis. Alternatively, use three shop-bought containers of a similar size. Sow individual ingredients in rows in the boxes to prevent the vigorous ones taking over and so that you can harvest them separately.

You will need

5 x 15 cm (2 x 6 in) lengths of timber, 12 m (40 ft)

Saw for cutting the planks

Drill for weatherproof screws

Heavy-duty black plastic liner

Heavy-duty staples and stapler

Utility knife

Water-based wood stain

Compost

5 packets of seeds: rocket, loose-leaf lettuce, parsley, spinach, mustard and mizuna (see page 126 for alternatives)

Fine mesh cover and cloche

Balanced all-purpose fertiliser

Planting your pots

1. Adapt the shape of the salad bar to fit your space, building the boxes in a straight line or L shape; the dimensions of 45 x 55 cm (18 x 22 in) for each box works well. Cut the wood to size and use screws to hold them together at the ends. Line the inside of the salad bar with heavy-duty plastic liners and secure in place with staples, then make some slits in them for drainage holes, using a utility knife. Paint the boxes with a water-based stain.

2. Fill the boxes with compost. You can fill the bottom with garden soil or garden compost, but you need fresh compost for the top 10–15 cm (4–6 in).

3. Sow one box in rows 10 cm (4 in) apart with 1–2 cm (½–¾ in) between seeds. Mizuna is often the most vigorous, so sow it at one end; rocket is often fast, so sow it at another end. Sow a box every two to three weeks for a continuous supply.

4. Water to keep the compost moist, and watch out for slugs and aphids. Cover with a cloche for a few weeks if there are cats around; later on, if flea beetles nibble holes in the rocket, use a fine mesh cover.

5. Cut the plants 2 cm (¾ in) above the soil, leaving a stump. If fed and watered, the stumps re-grow in three to four weeks; repeat up to three times.

Strawberry Delight

An early variety of June-bearing strawberries with violas planted underneath will provide a pretty spring flower combination as well as tasty, freshly picked summer strawberries. This planting uses a long but lightweight rectangular planter to accommodate five strawberry plants. Alternatively, plant up to six rooted runners into a growing bag placed on a low wall or outdoor table.

You will need

Plastic planter, 75 x 25 x 25 cm (30 x 10 x 10 in)

Drainage material such as crocks or gravel

Empty 7.5 cm (3 in) plastic flowerpot

Loam-based potting mix

5 'Elsanta' (or other early variety, such as 'Earliglow') potted strawberry plants in spring

10 violas

Straw (optional)

Tomato fertiliser

Planting your pot

1. Add a drainage layer to the base of the planter, using crocks or gravel. Position an empty flowerpot, right way up, in the middle; you will use it to quickly deliver water to the roots.

2. Add the compost, firming it in well – including into the corners – as you fill the container. This will reduce any settling when it is watered, otherwise the plants will sink. Plant the strawberries so the crown of the plant is just above the compost surface.

3. Water carefully to avoid wetting the flowers; during heavy rain, provide shelter for the flowers to prevent grey mould developing, which can infect the flowers and fruit. Start applying a tomato fertiliser once the plants start to flower.

4. As the strawberries ripen, keep them clean by tucking some straw under the fruit near the surface of the compost. Pick the strawberries every day or every other day.

Eton mess

Rinse 225 g (8 oz) strawberries, remove the stalks and cut in half or quarters, depending on their size. Put the strawberries in a bowl, sprinkle with 1 tablespoon sugar and stir to mix, crushing a few berries against the sides. Chill. Meanwhile, whip 500 ml (17 fl oz) double cream until it forms soft peaks. Crumble 6 plain meringues into the cream, then mix in the chilled strawberries and stir gently. Pile into individual pudding bowls and serve.

Shady Ladies

Although a sunny site is the most productive for the majority of plants, many people have shady areas in their outdoor space. But as long as these have sun for part of the day or get dappled shade, they can be productive sites, too. This container was started in early spring with tulips, French tarragon and young lettuces. After flowering, the tulips were removed and replaced with begonias.

You will need

Rectangular wooden planter, 30 x 38 x 20 cm (12 x 15 x 8 in)

Drill (optional)

Plastic liner

Utility knife

Drainage material such as crocks or pebbles

Compost

1 French tarragon plant

6 potted tulip plants

2 small red lettuce plants (any type, but loose-leaf lettuce would be best)

2 begonia plants with red flowers

Planting your pot

1. Drill drainage holes in the planter, if necessary. Next, position the liner inside the planter, and cut some slits in the liner for drainage. Add the drainage material and fill the planter with the compost.

2. Plant the French tarragon along the back edge of the planter, in the middle, then plant the tulips on either side of it for spring colour. Plant young red lettuce plants along the front edge.

3. The planter can be placed at the front of a border; rest it on a paving slab to help preserve the wood from the damp ground.

4. After the tulip flowers have died back, remove the plants, roots and all, and fill the spaces with red begonias. The lettuces and tarragon will grow to fill the space.

5. Harvest the lettuces and tarragon as needed. More young lettuce plants can be added. Keep the compost just moist; there is no need to fertilise.

6. At the end of the season you will still have the tarragon; you can let it continue to grow and fill the container.

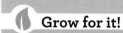

Grow for it!

More shade-tolerant plants

Herbs Chervil, chives, lemon balm, mint

Vegetables Beetroot, kale, radish, spinach

Flowers Impatiens, nasturtium, violas

Courgette Feast

The humble courgette has been given a makeover by choosing a yellow variety and planting it in a feature container along with some bright edible flowers. This copper-blue 'Bell Jar' is made of fibreglass and is based on a design by sculptor Bill Harling. It forms the centrepiece within a small herb-growing area, but the planting would work equally well in a lined plastic laundry basket.

You will need

Blue fibreglass flowerpot,
  50 cm (20 in) in diameter

Drainage material

Compost

2 bush yellow courgette plants

3 nasturtium plants or seeds

2 blue-flowered borage plants

Tomato fertiliser

 Grow for it!

Edible flowers

Borage Slight cucumber flavour but mainly used as a garnish for its pretty flowers.

Nasturtium The pepper-flavoured flowers add colour to salads, rice and pasta dishes.

Courgette Used to hold a soft stuffing that is spooned in, or dip them in batter and fry.

Planting your pot

1. You can raise the flowerpot on bricks so it emerges from the surrounding plants. Fill the bottom one-third to one-half of the pot with drainage material or a mixture of drainage material and garden soil, then add fresh compost.

2. Make a slight mound in the centre of the pot. When there is no danger of frost, plant two hardened-off courgette plants in the centre. Let the plants become established, taking care to water the surrounding soil, not the stems or foliage.

3. Arrange the nasturtium plants around the rim or insert seeds into the surface. Choose a variety with variegated foliage as well as a range of orange and red flowers such as 'Alaska'.

4. Once the other plants are well established, insert the borage to fill any gaps. All three plants have edible flowers and attract beneficial insects.

5. As the courgettes form, remove any shrivelled blooms. Apply a tomato fertiliser and increase watering. Cut back the nasturtiums and borage if they start to look straggly.

Pasta with courgette

Cook 450 g (1 lb) of tagliatelle or fettuccini according to packet instructions. Reserve and set aside 125 ml (4 fl oz) cooking liquid. Meanwhile, heat 2 tablespoons olive oil in a saucepan over a medium-high heat. Add 1 thinly sliced shallot and sauté for 2–3 minutes, stirring often. Add 2 courgettes cut into cubes and sauté for 3–4 minutes. Add the pasta to the saucepan, along with half the reserved cooking liquid, toss to coat the noodles and cook for 1–2 minutes. Season to taste with salt and ground black pepper, turn off the heat and stir in 175 g (6 oz) crumbled goat's cheese and grated zest from 1 lemon.

Pick of the Day

From this one container, you will have a long season of regular pickings that will provide you with fresh, flavoursome herbs through the seasons and a summer salad of lettuce and tomatoes. By using a square container, you can space the plantings in three 'rows', packing in a surprising amount. The planting contains a mixture of hardy and tender subjects, with some perennials and some annuals.

You will need

Square fibreglass planter,
   40 x 40 x 40 cm
   (16 x 16 x 16 in)

Drainage material such as
   crocks, gravel or polystyrene
   packing peanuts

Multipurpose compost

1 small cherry tomato plant

1 dwarf lavender plant

1 purple-leaved basil plant

4 small green loose-leaf lettuces

1 chive plant

1 oregano plant

Tomato fertiliser

Planting your pot

1. Put in about 5 cm (2 in) of drainage material, then add the compost, pushing plenty of compost into each corner.

2. Start with the tomato, because depending on its size, you may need to adjust the number and position of the other plants. Plant it in one corner; it may need up to one-quarter of the planter. Plant the other corners with the lavender, basil, oregano and chives. If the clump of chives is large, divide it into smaller sections.

3. Now fill in the gaps with small lettuces, perhaps three in the middle row and one between the tomato and basil. Keep spare plants in separate pots for replacements later on.

4. First cut the chive and oregano foliage; they are tasty when they are young and it keeps the plants small. Pick the lavender flowers when in bud. Cut the loose-leaf lettuces as you need them. Later, the chives and oregano will flower; you can eat the petals.

5. When flowering, start to feed the tomato plant. Pick ripe tomatoes and the basil. Remove the lettuces when they begin to set seed in summer. In autumn, remove the tomato and basil plants.

 Grow for it!

Alternative colours

Each of the six subjects in the recipe has alternatives in different colours, so there are many colour combinations. Cherry tomatoes are also available with yellow or orange fruits, which can be paired with a red-leaved lettuce and a green-leaved Genovese basil. A specialist herb nursery can supply, for example, white-flowered chives, golden oregano and a paler mauve lavender.

Bouquet Garni Box

A bouquet garni is a small bundle of different herbs tied together or tied inside a muslin bag and added to slow-cooking meat dishes and stews. The herbs in this planting provide more than enough leaves for the traditional bouquet garni of bay leaf, parsley and thyme. And there are other herbs to make it a complete cook's package: sage (for pork), rosemary (for lamb) and tarragon (for poultry and fish).

You will need

1 recycled packing crate, 36 x 53 cm (14 x 21 in), 25 cm (10 in) deep

Two 60 cm (2 ft) hessian squares

45 x 64 cm (18 x 25 in) piece of black flexible pond liner from an aquatic store

Utility knife

Drainage material such as crocks or polystyrene packing peanuts

Compost with perlite mixed in

1 small bay tree (Laurus nobilis)

1 prostrate rosemary plant

1 flat-leaf parsley plant

1 French tarragon plant

1 sage plant

1 golden-leaved thyme plant

1 silver-leaved thyme plant

Planting your pot

1. Line the crate with the hessian, then cover the base with the pond liner, allowing it to extend a few centimetres up the sides. Make some drainage slits in the pond liner. Add a 5 cm (2 in) layer of a lightweight drainage material.

2. Woody herbs grow better in a loam-based compost, but to keep this planting portable, use a lightweight compost with perlite added for drainage. The bay tree is the most valuable and you can replant it in its own container of loam-based compost at the end of the season and move it indoors for winter.

3. Position the bay tree in the centre and pack compost around it. Space out the other herbs, with three at the back and three at the front. We have used large pots of herbs for instant cover, but you can use smaller pots and mulch the spaces in between with gravel.

4. There are plenty of herbs to provide fresh leaves from spring to autumn. Because woody herbs with tough leaves (bay, sage, rosemary and thyme) dry well (see 'Drying herbs', right), preserve them at their peak in midsummer.

Drying herbs

A microwave oven speeds up the drying process. Harvest the leaves before the plant flowers and in the morning after the dew has dried. Clean the leaves, removing any discoloured, dirty or diseased ones. Lay them out on a single layer of two sheets of kitchen paper. Microwave for 2 minutes, check and, if not dry, microwave again for 30 seconds. Using clean, dry hands, crumble the leaves into clean, dry screw-top jars labelled with the herb and date. Bay leaves are best in a wide-neck jar and stored whole, not crumbled.

Sweet Sisters

Here's a modern recipe inspired by the traditional 'three sisters' planting of sweetcorn, beans and squash practised by Native Americans. Sweetcorn makes an impressive foliage feature, but here we used sweet potato instead of squash because sweet potato tubers require less space in the pot. A plastic container is ideal because it is large, yet light enough to be moved and to tip out the tubers.

You will need

Heavy-duty plastic container, 45 cm (18 in) in diameter, 40 cm (16 in) deep

Drill for holes

Drainage material such as a few crocks or polystyrene packing peanuts

Compost

5 sweetcorn seeds

4 dwarf bean seeds (or 4 small sweet pepper plants)

1 potted sweet potato plant

5 small nasturtium plants or seeds

Tomato fertiliser (if growing pepper plants)

Planting your pot

1. You need a pot that is deep and can hold at least five sweetcorn plants (to improve pollination). Make drainage holes in the pot. Fill the base with a drainage layer. Add the compost, mounding it in the centre and firming down gently.

2. All the vegetables are tender and cannot be planted outside until after the last frost. Start the beans and sweetcorn in individual coir pots in a light, frost-free place in spring; buy a potted sweet potato plant.

3. Plant the sweet potato in the centre of the mound, plant the sweetcorn around it, then add the beans or peppers. Finally, add the nasturtiums at the edge of the planter as either potted plants or seeds. Keep the pot in a warm, sheltered place; the sweetcorn may need support. Apply organic slug pellets.

4. The nasturtiums add early colour and some edible flowers; remove them later if they get too straggly in hot weather. When the beans start to crop, pick them regularly for a steady supply. If you are growing sweet peppers, they will appear later and will benefit from a tomato fertiliser.

5. Harvest the cobs when the silks start to turn brown; remove the sweetcorn plants when depleted. Tip out and harvest the sweet potatoes 100–110 days after planting. The tubers will be small, so they won't store well for long.

Flavours to Savour

From this one pot you will have refreshing aniseed leaf bases and foliage, celery-flavoured stems and leaves for soups or stock, and hot, spicy salad leaves. All need a moist, rich soil, so a large, thick terracotta flowerpot is used to hold plenty of compost. The green foliage and terracotta pot form a calm backdrop in the garden, and there are plenty of flavours for the cook.

You will need

Terracotta flowerpot, 45 cm (18 in) in diameter, 30 cm (12 in) deep

Heavy-duty plastic liner and utility knife (depending on choice of flowerpot)

Drainage material such as crocks

Rich compost

3 celery plants

3 Florence fennel plants

3 land cress plants (or use watercress, see 'Watercress', right)

Balanced all-purpose fertiliser

Planting your pot

1. The flowerpot should be thick and heavy, so place it in its final location before filling with the drainage material and a moisture-retentive, rich compost. If you use a terracotta flowerpot with thinner sides, first line it with heavy-duty black plastic and cut some slits in it at the base for drainage holes.

2. Start by positioning the young fennel plants in the centre of the pot, then add the young celery plants and finish with some land cress or watercress plants.

3. Check the container daily and, if needed, water to keep the compost moist. The celery, in particular, needs fertilising with a balanced all-purpose fertiliser within a few weeks of planting and every few weeks afterwards.

4. The land cress will be ready first in early summer; cut with scissors as required. The Florence fennel will form small swollen leaf bases by the end of the summer. Cut these off at the base; leave the roots, which will grow some more foliage that can then be used as you would herb fennel. The celery will produce thin stems, which will be slightly blanched by the land cress.

 Grow for it!

Watercress

You can grow watercress from seed in the spring or take a cutting from a bunch of watercress and root it in a small pot of compost. Keep it damp until it is growing well, then plant outside into the final container. Keep it watered and fertilised. Remove any flowers and cut leaves as you need them.

Citrus Sense

A citrus plant, with its heady, scented flowers and juicy fruit, will give a patio a Mediterranean feeling, especially if you use a Versailles-style planter. It is named after a type of wooden box used at Versailles Palace in France for plants that spent summer on the terrace and winter inside. Lemons are practical for small patios in warm spots; even a small plant 90 cm (3 ft) tall will yield a large number of fruit.

You will need

Wooden Versailles planter,
   30 x 38 x 38 cm
   (12 x 15 x 15 in)

Heavy-duty liner

Utility knife

Citrus compost (or a loam-based
   mix with added horticultural grit
   to improve drainage)

1 grafted lemon tree (Citrus limon)

4 lemon variegated thyme plants

Citrus fertiliser

Planting your pot

1. Position the liner (generally supplied with the planter) and cut some drainage holes in it. Add some citrus compost, usually available online.

2. Select a lemon tree with fruit already forming; the fruit will grow and ripen slowly but will hang on the tree until you are ready to use them. Remove the plant from its original pot, place it carefully in the centre of the planter, and fill it with compost. Any underplanting needs to be drought-tolerant and discrete such as thyme; plant one in each corner.

3. Place the planter in a light, sheltered position. Allow the compost to dry out a little between watering. Feed with a citrus fertiliser, following the manufacturer's instructions. Thin out fruitlets so there is only one fruit per cluster. Trim the thyme if it gets straggly.

4. Citrus plants can sit outside from early summer to early autumn but they need to overwinter in a conservatory or somewhere with a minimum temperature of 7°C (45°F). Potted citrus plants are heavy; to move one use a plant trolley or use a planter supplied with castors.

Preserved lemons

Use the juice from preserved lemons to flavour salad dressings, soups, and meat, fish or chicken sauces. Quarter 5 lemons almost to the base, sprinkle salt on the exposed flesh and reshape the fruit. Pack the lemons into a sterilised jar in layers with 55 g (2 oz) salt, 1 tablespoon olive oil, 1 cinnamon stick, 3 cloves, 4 black peppercorns, 6 coriander seeds and 2 bay leaves between the layers. Press the lemons to release their juices, adding freshly squeezed lemon juice to cover them. Seal the jar and keep it in a warm place for 30 days, shaking the jar every day. They will keep for 6 months; refrigerate after opening.

Fire Pit

A kadai is an Indian circular, metal pot used over a fire to cook for large get-togethers such as weddings and festivals. Recycled kadai may be imported and used outside on low stands as barbecues or plant holders. This kadai has been planted with an impromptu display of edibles in a vibrant display of yellow, purple, orange and red.

You will need

Recycled kadai (available online, or an old, shallow metal container), 80 cm (32 in) in diameter

Plastic liner or newspaper

3 yellow sweet pepper plants with supporting bamboo canes

2 large pots of purple-flowered thyme plants

2 large pots of chive plants

2 large pots of parsley plants

2 large pots of coriander plants

Packing material such as newspaper or polystyrene packing peanuts (optional)

Compost

12 pots of nasturtium plants

Drainage material such as polystyrene packing peanuts (optional)

Planting your pot

1. For a temporary display to act as a centrepiece, line the container with plastic or newspaper to protect the surface. Water all the plants well beforehand. Place the pots of sweet peppers in the centre – look for ones with supporting bamboo canes in place or insert your own.

2. Arrange the herbs in a circle around the sweet peppers; you can leave them in their pots and raise the height up with newspaper or packing peanuts. Finish off with a layer of compost to hide the packing material.

3. Set out the nasturtiums in pots around the edge and cover with compost. You can plan ahead and grow these from seed by planting them into small flowerpots in early spring.

4. The plants will last for a couple of days without watering. By then you will need to water directly into the pots.

5. If you want a more permanent display, put drainage material into the base of the kadai before adding some compost, then remove the plants from their pots and plant, firming down more compost around them. You may want to remove the nasturtiums once they start to look straggly.

Crops in Corners

Square planters add a formal touch and are versatile. They are also ideal for making the most use of space in corners. Plus they are beautiful as centrepieces on their own, or set out with similar planters to form an edge to a patio area. In this case, a large pepper plant takes centre stage, with a small cherry tomato plant, foliage herbs and summer bedding positioned underneath to create a vibrant planting.

You will need

Fibreglass planter, 33 cm (13 in) square and deep

Drill

Drainage material such as crocks, gravel or polystyrene packing peanuts

Compost

1 pepper plant, either sweet or hot

2 calibrachoa plants

1 small cherry tomato plant

1 flat-leaf parsley plant

1 lemon-scented thyme plant

Tomato fertiliser

Planting your pot

1. Drill drainage holes in the planter, then add plenty of drainage material and compost. Make sure you push plenty of compost into each corner.

2. The pepper, tomato and bedding plants are frost-sensitive, so do not plant outside until all danger of frost has passed and the plants have been hardened off.

3. Start with the pepper plant; depending on its size, you may need to adjust the number and position of the other plants. Plant the pepper off-centre into a corner, then plant a calibrachoa on each side, with the plants cascading out. Next, plant the tomato plant and herbs.

4. The pepper and tomato plants may need supporting canes. Place in a warm, sunny spot. Start cutting the herb foliage first; the leaves are more tasty when young and cutting keeps the plants producing leaves. Feed with a tomato fertiliser to promote fruiting on the tomato and pepper plants as well as flowers on the calibrachoa. Pick the tomatoes and peppers when ripe.

No-cook mixed pickle

It is easy to pickle firm-textured vegetables such as cauliflower, cucumbers, green beans, baby onions and peppers. Prepare the vegetables as you would for a recipe, trimming and cutting into florets, slices or wedges. Soak them for 1–2 days in 450 g (1 lb) salt mixed with 4.5 litres (7½ pints) water. Drain the vegetables, rinse and dry thoroughly. Pack the vegetables in a sterilised, airtight container, leaving a 2.5 cm (1 in) gap at the top; cover completely with a herb or spice vinegar, mixed with sugar to taste. Place a disc of greaseproof paper and clingfilm on top to seal, then tightly secure the lid. Store in the refrigerator for up to 3 months.

Royal Potatoes

Growing your own potatoes in pots or bags is popular because you don't need a vegetable garden, and it avoids diseases that can be picked up from garden soil. It is a fun project to do with children. This planting uses different varieties to provide a mixture of red, white and blue potatoes, but you can, of course, use any potato variety.

You will need

1 terracotta flowerpot, 50 cm (20 in) in diameter, 45 cm (18 in) deep

Drainage material such as gravel or packing peanuts

Rich compost

3 sprouted seed potatoes (see Potatoes, pages 132–133), 1 each of a red-, white- and blue-flesh variety

Garden fleece

Balanced all-purpose fertiliser

Planting your pot

1. In mild areas, or if you have a light and frost-free greenhouse or conservatory, start planting the pot in early spring. If you cannot guarantee the plants will be frost-free, wait until mid- to late spring. Prepare your containers. Line the base with a layer of gravel or packing peanuts to help drainage. Half-fill the containers with compost.

2. Plant the sprouted seed potatoes and cover with compost. As the plants grow, add more compost to just cover the growing tips. If frost is forecast, cover the container with a double layer of garden fleece or bring it indoors.

3. Keep the compost moist, but not too wet or the potatoes will rot. Keep adding compost until it almost reaches the rim of the container. Water regularly and apply a balanced all-purpose fertiliser every few weeks.

4. When the plants start to bloom, the tubers will be forming. When there are plenty of flowers, push your hand into the compost and feel for tubers. If several are the size of a hen's egg, pull them out; leave the plants to produce more. When the foliage dies down, turn out the compost and collect the tubers.

Going UP!

Vertical gardening is all about finding opportunities to grow edibles using the space above. Conventional containers can be turned into havens for vegetables, with window boxes becoming fresh salad bars and hanging baskets making a home for tomatoes. You can transform bare walls and fences into productive areas, thanks to planting pouches or pockets that are ideal for planting with a selection of different crops. Last but not least, there is nothing like climbing beans to fill vertical space productively, so if you have a house, garage or shed wall facing the sun, put up a trellis or netting and get growing!

77

Sunshine in a Box

Sunflowers bring a smile to everyone, and they brighten up a windowsill. Using a neutral wooden window box lets you decorate or customise the planting. The harvest from the beans will be modest, but their flowers will add a splash of colour; make sure you add some herbs to the planter as an edging. The dried sunflower heads are a natural food for birds.

You will need

Wooden window box,
   60 x 25 x 20 cm
   (24 x 10 x 8 in)

Drill for drainage holes, if
   necessary, and for fittings

Plastic liner

Utility knife

Compost

1–3 dwarf sunflower plants

6–8 dwarf runner bean plants
   such as 'Hestia'

4 small, yellow-variegated
   thyme plants

Support fittings such as
   screws or brackets

Balanced all-purpose fertiliser

Planting your pot

1. Drill drainage holes into the window box, if necessary. Next, position the liner and cut some slits in it for drainage (but first see Step 5 below). Fill the window box with the compost.

2. Plant the sunflower in the centre of the box – choose a dwarf variety that will do better in a confined space. The sunflower will need regular watering and feeding, so you might want a few replacements to hand.

3. Plant the beans on either side of the sunflower. Although you are using a small variety, the plants may still need a little support in windy locations. Plant the beans close together so they will support themselves, but you can also insert some short canes or pea sticks.

4. Fill in the front edge with a low-growing herb such as thyme; yellow-variegated thyme picks up the sunflower's yellow petals, and when it blooms, it will have small mauve flowers.

5. Lift the box into position and fix it. The fittings you use will depend on the type of windowsill and window box. You can hold the box in place by drilling through it and attaching it to the sill with screws. In this case, do so before planting the box; use a stiff liner so you can plant into it, then fix it in place.

Stepping Out with Basil

Basil delivers a heady aroma and a taste of the Mediterranean in a neat package. Besides the traditional green-leaved basil, there are varieties with smaller or colourful leaves, ornamental flowers and spicy flavours. Here are the best of each to make the perfect herbal treat for an urban dweller. Basil doesn't cope with cold, damp or root disturbance, so buy potted plants.

You will need

3 lime-green metal containers, 15 cm (6 in) in diameter

1 basil 'Sweet Genovese'

1 basil 'Aristotle'

1 purple-leaved basil plant

Balanced all-purpose fertiliser

* The plants pictured here are on a fire escape, but please note they should not be left unsecured on steps, where they could fall off. And they should not block an emergency exit.

Planting your pots

1. Use potted plants in 13 cm (5 in) diameter pots that fit in the metal containers. For basil plants sold in 9 cm (3½ in) pots, you can transfer them into a 13 cm (5 in) pot and pinch out the plants' growing tips to encourage bushiness, or use two plants per 13 cm (5 in) pot.

2. Put each potted plant into a metal container; these do not have drainage holes, so you need to lift out the inner pot daily and pour out any water at the base of the metal container. You can also place basil on a windowsill, indoors or outside.

3. The plants need some watering, and if you harvest large-leaved types heavily, apply a balanced all-purpose fertiliser.

4. 'Sweet Genovese' is the one to pick and eat for the classic flavour. 'Aristotle' has small leaves and is neat; trim with scissors to use as a pretty garnish. You can use basil with colourful leaves for cooking, but they are also ornamental, especially when the lilac flowers appear.

Aromatic roasted tomatoes

Preheat the oven to 190°C (375°F/Gas Mark 5). Grease an ovenproof dish with 1 tablespoon olive oil. Core 900 g (2 lb) tomatoes, then cut into wedges. Put the tomatoes, cut side up, in the dish. Break up 1 head of garlic into cloves and scatter around the tomatoes. Cut 6 sprigs basil and tuck between the tomatoes, then sprinkle with salt and ground black pepper. Drizzle 2 tablespoons olive oil over the tomatoes. Roast for 30 minutes, until the tomatoes are lightly charred on the outside. Sprinkle with 2 tablespoons freshly torn basil leaves and serve.

Salsa Box

Just as there are many recipes for salsa, this planting is equally flexible, depending on how hot you like your flavours. The main two plants are a tomato and a pepper. Look for compact varieties suitable for a small pot, then choose a sweet pepper or chilli. The 'African Blue' basil looks great in flower, but if you can't find one, any small green basil, coriander or thyme will work, too.

You will need

Wooden or plastic window box, 60 cm (24 in) long, 15 cm (6 in) wide and deep

Drill for drainage holes and for securing the bracket

Bracket and screws for a wooden balcony

Water-based stain (optional)

Liner, stiff or flexible

Drainage material such as crocks or gravel

Compost

1 bush red pepper plant (sweet pepper or chilli)

1 tomato plant (tumbler type with medium fruit)

1 ornamental basil 'African Blue'

2 small-leaved basil plants

2 lemon thyme plants or coriander plants

Tomato fertiliser

Planting your pot

1. All the plants are tender, so keep them in a light, frost-free place and harden off well. The advantage of planting into a stiff liner is you can have another liner with a spring planting in the box, then swap them over in early summer when this planting will be ready.

2. Add drainage holes to the box, and apply a water-based stain if needed. Secure the window box to the balcony. Put the plants into a stiff liner and place the liner in the box; alternatively, position the liner before adding the plants. In either case, first add a layer of drainage material and compost before adding the plants.

3. Position the pepper at one end of the box and the tomato at the other end; add the basil near the tomato to give height. Fill any gaps with small green herbs. If the box will be viewed from all sides, take this into account when planting.

4. Keep the compost moist, and give the pepper and tomato plants a tomato fertiliser to encourage a productive crop.

Salsa

Cut 4 small tomatoes in half crossways, squeeze out the seeds and dice. Put them into a bowl with 1 finely chopped garlic clove, 1 seeded and diced sweet red pepper, the juice of half a lime, ½ teaspoon salt and 1 teaspoon thyme leaves. Stir to blend. For a hot salsa, add 1 small hot chilli, deseeded and finely chopped. Stir again, then cover and let the flavours blend together for at least 30 minutes before serving.

Goldfinger's Bean Basket

These dwarf bean plants are prolific croppers and perfect for containers that are lifted off the ground. Unlike when these plants are grown in the ground, the beans will not be splashed with mud, and they will be easier to pick. This well-prepared hanging basket is filled with eye-catching yellow beans, and there is extra colour from fresh frilly leaved red lettuce.

You will need

Hanging basket, with open sides, 35 cm (14 in) in diameter

Loose liner

Piece of plastic sheet for lining base of the basket

Compost

Water-retaining granules (in dry regions)

5–6 dwarf bean plants, any yellow pod variety

3 red loose-leaf lettuce plants

Bracket and screws

Garden fleece

Secateurs

Planting your pot

1. Line the base of the basket with a loose basket liner, then put in a piece of plastic sheeting, working up from the base of the basket.

2. Use a compost that has water-retaining granules already mixed in it, or sprinkle on the granules as instructed on the packet and mix in well. Half-fill the basket with compost.

3. Insert three small bean plants around the sides of the basket, then fill it up with compost, firming down gently around the roots. Young, small plants are easier to handle than bigger plants, but do so carefully because beans dislike being transplanted. Plant the top of the basket with the remaining two or three bean plants, plus three small lettuce plants.

4. The bean plants will be sensitive to frost, so be aware of the last frost dates and make sure plants are hardened off well. Protect the plants with garden fleece, if necessary. Hang the basket in a sunny, sheltered position. Avoid a windy site. Check the basket daily to make sure the compost is moist.

5. Harvest the lettuces little and often. Cut off the beans with secateurs instead of pulling them; tugging on the beans can dislodge the plant. Harvest the beans little and often to encourage more beans to form.

Pick and Mix

This vertical planter with planting pockets is easy to fill and will provide a variety of herbs for cooking. Position it outside the kitchen door on a sunny surface. Almost any edible plant sold in small pots can be used, but we chose long-lasting foliage herbs. To get the horizontal striped effect, keep the same plant type in each row, and vary the colours and textures between rows.

You will need

1 planting pouch, with separate planting pockets arranged in pairs

Fixings (wall anchors and galvanised screws)

Drill or screwdriver for securing the fixings

Compost

2–4 winter savory or prostrate rosemary plants

2–4 curly parsley plants

2–4 variegated sage plants

2–4 yellow pansies or violas*

* If you want these as edible plants, ask the supplier if they have been sprayed with chemicals. Or grow your own organically from seed.

Planting your pot

1. Attach the planter to the wall as directed on the packet instructions. Choose a height that is convenient for you to water and harvest, but also take into account how much light there is for plant growth.

2. Plants in small 7.5 cm (3 in) diameter pots are the easiest to use for this type of planter. Water the plants well before planting. You can use one plant per pocket, adding in extra compost and allowing room for the plant to fill out. Or to provide an instant finished look, plant two plants per pocket, adding as much compost as you can.

3. When adding extra compost, take time to fill the corners. However, leave a gap at the top so when the pockets are watered, the compost is not washed out. Water the compost so it is barely moist. Start harvesting as soon as the plants are well established.

4. Because each type of plant has its own root area, it is easy to replace them without disturbing other plants.

 Grow for it!

Planting pouches

Pouches and other similar planters, where plants are inserted through slits in fabric or plastic, are easier to plant with small plug plants. For the best results, keep the pouch or planter lying flat for 1 or 2 weeks, so the roots can get established, then hang it up in place. This prevents water dislodging the young plants.

Sunny Window Box

There are flavours a plenty in this small window box, yet it is decorative, too. The purple foliage is balanced by the softer green of the tarragon and thyme. Many of the herbs can be left to flower or pinched out and trimmed so there are more leaves to harvest. The planting needs a warm, sunny spot. However, it is drought-tolerant, apart from the purple shiso, which wilts rapidly but will recover.

You will need

Wooden window box, 60 cm (24 in) long, 20 cm (8 in) wide and 23 cm (9 in) deep

Drill for drainage holes and securing the bracket

Bracket and screws for a wooden balcony

Liner (flexible)

Utility knife

Drainage material such as crocks, gravel or polystyrene packing peanuts

Compost

1 purple shiso (also known as perilla or Japanese basil; *Perilla frutescens purpurascens*)

1 French tarragon plant

1 purple basil plant

3 basil plants

4 thyme plants

Planting your pot

1. Drill drainage holes in the base of the box, and fix the box and bracket to the balcony or fence. Put in the flexible liner, make some drainage slits with the knife and fill with the drainage material, followed by the compost.

2. Put the tallest plant (in this case the purple shiso) in the centre of the box. Select the next two tallest plants, a basil and tarragon, and plant one at each end of the box.

3. Fill any remaining gaps with the remaining plants. Gaps at the back of the planter can be filled with a basil with flower spikes. The purple basil can be placed in front of the taller basil plants and one of the thyme plants at the other end of the window box in front of the tarragon. Small plants of thyme form a neat edge under the purple shiso. Firm the plants in well, taking care to push plenty of compost into the corners of the box.

4. Pick and use the leaves as required, leaving the basil to provide the flowers. The planting will need watering but not feeding.

Tarragon vinegar

Capture the subtle flavour of tarragon by making a vinegar to add to salad dressings, fish or chicken. Open a 500 ml (16 fl oz) screw-top bottle of white wine vinegar, pour off some of the vinegar, then push in a few sprigs of young tarragon leaves and stems. Fill with vinegar, replace the lid and shake. Within a month, the vinegar will have a subtle flavour. Or, for a stronger flavour, strip off a handful of leaves from their stems. Put in a clean, dry, empty jar. Cover with white wine vinegar, replace the lid and shake. After a month, strain the vinegar and return it, minus the leaves, to the jar. Remember to label it.

Tomato Catch-up

Here is a quick and easy way to plant and grow tomatoes and herbs. All the ingredients can be bought as potted plants in early summer and planted into the top of the basket. A 35 cm (14 in) diameter basket provides enough compost for the plants, and it needs less regular watering than a smaller basket. The herbs can be varied, but look for low-growing varieties.

You will need

Hanging basket, with open sides, 35 cm (14 in) in diameter

Coco fibre liner for 35 cm (14 in) basket

Plastic saucer or piece of flexible plastic

Compost

1 tumbler-type tomato plant

1 compact oregano plant

2 curly parsley plants

1 winter savory plant

1 prostrate rosemary plant

Bracket for a 35 cm (14 in) basket and screws

Drill or screwdriver for fixing the bracket

Tomato fertiliser

Planting your pot

1. Insert the liner into the base of the basket, then put it on a saucer or piece of plastic to help retain moisture.

2. Fill the basket two-thirds full with compost, firming gently as you fill.

3. Plant the tomato plant at the top of the basket, making sure it is in the centre, and firm down gently. Continue to pack compost around the roots; the plant should be at the same depth that it was in its original pot. Leave a 2.5 cm (1 in) gap between the top of the compost and the top of the basket.

4. Retain any small supports that came with the tomato plant to help lift the stems above the compost. Position the small herb plants around the rim of the basket and firm in gently. The herbs are hardy but the tomato is frost-sensitive, so wait until after the last frost and harden off well before hanging up on a bracket positioned outside in a sunny and sheltered spot.

5. Check the basket daily to make sure the compost is moist, and use a tomato fertiliser as directed on the packet; feeding starts four weeks after planting and then weekly or biweekly thereafter.

6. Harvest the herb leaves little and often, snipping off leaves with scissors.

Windowsill Pesto

Who would guess this elegant green and white summer planting could also provide enough basil for a quick home-made pesto? There are four different herbs within this small window box, but it is the white cascading petunias that catch the eye. The planting area is small so, if possible, make a pair of these window boxes to increase your harvest, or adjust quantities to fit a larger box.

You will need

Faux lead window box (fibreglass), 60 cm (24 in) long, 20 cm (8 in) wide and deep

Drill for drainage holes (optional)

Drainage material such as crocks, gravel or polystyrene packing peanuts

Compost

4–5 sweet or Genovese basil plants

2 basil plants with large leaves

2 garlic chive plants

1 oregano plant

2 white trailing petunia plants

Planting your pot

1. Make drainage holes in the box if there are none, put in the drainage material and fill with compost.

2. This window box is narrow, so look for young herbs in small pots or grow them yourself from seed.

3. Position the plants before planting; it will be easier to start with the petunias at each end and then fill in with the smaller plants. Plant the oregano in the centre along the back edge, with a garlic chive on either side, and fill in with large-leaved basil. Plant the sweet basil in front.

4. The petunia and basil are tender; keep them in a light, frost-free place and harden off well.

5. Keep the compost barely moist. Start picking the oregano and chive leaves first, then pick the basil once the plants are growing well. If left alone, all will flower. To keep the planting looking its best, cut the garlic chive leaves down to the base instead of snipping the ends.

Quick pesto

Toast 65 g (2¼ oz) pine kernels in a dry frying pan over a medium-high heat, stirring often, for a few minutes until golden. Take care not to let them burn. Leave to cool. Add them to the bowl of a food processor with 1 garlic clove, 50 g (1¾ oz) loosely packed basil leaves and 45 g (1½ oz) grated Parmesan cheese. Chop in bursts until the leaves are shredded, then gradually pour in 60 ml (2 fl oz) olive oil with the motor running. It should be thick and smooth. If the pesto looks dry, stir in a little more olive oil. Taste and add salt and ground black pepper, if necessary.

Climbing High

A sunny surface, such as the back of a fence, garage or shed, just needs a support and a deep container. You will then be set to grow productive, attractive climbing beans. To keep the planter looking neat, there is a row of small-leaved, compact basil plants forming an edible topiary, which can be clipped into shape as you harvest them. At each end of the planter, a touch of colour comes from bright red begonias.

You will need

Plastic planter, 70 cm (28 in) long, 30 cm (12 in) wide and deep

Drill for making drainage holes (optional)

Wooden trellis or bean netting, 2 m (6 ft) high, 70 cm (28 in) wide

Galvanised screws and drill or screwdriver to secure the support

Drainage material such as gravel or polystyrene packing peanuts

Rich compost

7 potted climbing bean plants

6 potted begonia plants with red flowers

10 potted small-leaved, compact basil plants

Soft garden twine or plant ties

Planting your pot

1. Drill drainage holes in the planter, if necessary. Check the position of the planter, then attach the support such as a trellis into place. Position the planter underneath the support and add a layer of drainage material. You can enrich the compost by mixing in well-rotted organic matter such as garden compost.

2. All the plants are frost sensitive so they cannot be planted in the final container until there is no danger of frost, and they have been completely hardened off.

3. Bean plants don't like disturbance, so handle them carefully. Line the bean plants along the back of the planter, spacing them 10 cm (4 in) apart. Young plants need help to cling to the support, so tie them in using soft garden twine – eventually the plants will wind around themselves.

4. Plant three begonias at each end of of the planter. The red flowers go well with the red-flowered varieties of climbing bean, but you can also team white begonias with white flowers and so on.

5. Protect the plants from slugs, wind and cold when they are young. Water well.

Dill Gherkins to Go

Cucumbers will do well outside in a container, if they are given support and a sunny, sheltered position. Choose an outdoor variety, either one for pickling – this will produce plenty of small fruit to pickle whole – or any other outdoor cucumber for salads. To flavour the cucumber in a salad or when pickling, use the growing tips of dill containing the developing flower, stem and leaves.

You will need

Terracotta flowerpot, 30 cm (12 in) in diameter, 30 cm (12 in) deep

Drainage material

Compost

Supports such as bamboo canes or an obelisk

Bush-type cucumber plant

3 dill plants

Garden twine

Tomato fertiliser

Knife or secateurs

Planting your pot

1. Put some drainage material in the base of the pot. Add compost, piling it into a slight mound in the centre of the pot. Insert a cane or another support. Plant the cucumber in the centre of the mound; this will prevent water rotting the plant and encourage the roots to grow down and seek moisture.

2. Plant young dill plants around the edge of the pot. For a constant supply of young growing tips, sow seeds little and often into small pots as replacements.

3. The young cucumber needs help to attach to the support, so tie on stems using garden twine – eventually, the plant will twine by itself. Cucumber plants are frost-sensitive, so harden off plants gradually before planting outside after there is no danger of frost (see page 107).

4. Water the compost carefully, at first sparingly because the cucumber stem and roots can rot. Later, once the plant is growing well, water regularly or install an automatic-drip irrigation system. About six weeks after planting, feed with a tomato fertiliser to promote fruiting. Keep an eye out for powdery mildew; remove and destroy any affected leaves.

5. Cut off the cucumbers at the stem, using a sharp knife or secateurs; do not pull them off, or you might dislodge the plant.

How to Grow

Once you have decided where to position the containers and selected some plants to try, it is time to make sure you have all the materials you need and get started. Growing plants in containers means you don't have to worry about the quality of the soil in the ground (or even the lack of it) – but container growing has its own challenges. Each individual plant has to deliver more in a smaller space – and it needs your help. In this chapter, you'll learn how to get seedlings and plants off to a healthy start and how to keep them that way.

Watering the Plants

All plants in containers will need a regular supply of water, so first choose your water source and decide how you will get it to the plants on a regular basis. This will influence the type, size, number and position of the containers you will use.

Watering is vital for plants, but watering them can also be a chore. When planning your plantings, think about how you will water your plants. Thinking ahead will make watering them easier.

Watering for a few plants

If you plan to grow just a few small to medium plants, one or two watering cans may be all you will need. The right watering can makes all the difference; look for one with a detachable brass rose, which fits on the end of the spout to break up the stream of water. This gives you three ways to water: with the rose holes pointing upwards for gently watering seedlings, the rose holes downwards for young plants and just the spout for quickly watering mature tomatoes or for filling drip trays or reservoirs. Carrying two 4-litre watering cans – one in each hand – is easier than one large 8-litre

The rose on a watering can has holes to break up the water to mimic raindrops.

watering can, and small watering cans can also be lifted up higher to water wall planters and window boxes.

You may want to consider products available to help reduce the need for watering, such as self-watering containers (see 'Choosing Containers', pages 102–103) and adding water-retaining crystals to the compost.

Tap water and storing water

An outside tap with a back-flow preventer, garden hosepipe or two and some attachments will let you create a watering system tailor-made to your space. For example, a four-way connector will divide the water supply so you can have two water supplies controlled by water timers, leaving separate access to water for manual watering. A wall-mounted reel that rolls up the hosepipe automatically is a great time-saver. If you are using a hosepipe to water plants directly, fit an adjustable spray attachment to control the spray. A watering lance attachment provides extra reach (about 75–90 cm/2½–3 ft) for hanging baskets and window boxes.

Collecting rainwater from the roof of any building – including sheds and garages – via gutters and storing it in a water butt is a good source of water. Raise the butt up on bricks or other building material so you can easily get a watering can under the tap at the base. The water butt needs a lid to keep insects and debris out; designs low enough that children can climb or fall into need child-proof lids.

Watering via drip feeds

An efficient way of watering is to have a series of hoses with microtubing that emit drips of water attached to each container. These drip irrigation systems are almost always used in conjunction with an automatic timer. You can either buy a kit of hoses, microtubing and connectors, set up the system and then position the containers around it according to what the kit can accommodate. Or you can decide what containers you want and where to place them, then measure what you need and order a custom-made system. Whichever method you choose, it is easy to install after a little planning and set-up time. It will be worth the effort in the time saved if you were to manually water the plants.

Avoiding extremes

Even if it rains you still need to check whether you need to water your plants, because the containers might not be directly in the rain or the leaves might direct the water away from the compost. Stick your finger down into the compost; if it feels damp, there is no need to water. Even automatic-drip irrigation systems need checking, because the holes can get blocked.

 Grow for it!

Holiday watering
- Ask a friend or neighbour to keep an eye on your plants to keep the compost moist.
- Invest in holiday watering systems with a reservoir of water connected to a wick or a network of hoses. These will keep the compost moist long enough for you to take a short break.
- Do not be tempted to leave plant pots in deep trays of water for days, because the compost will become sodden and the roots will die.

If you find that watering a number of large plantings with a watering can is time-consuming, a hosepipe with a spray attachment is a good option.

Plants also die if their roots are in waterlogged compost. Be wary of planting small plants in large pots and then overwatering. If you use trays under pots, make sure the pots are not sitting in standing water. Pots may not have drainage holes or the holes might be insufficient. In addition to adding drainage holes, add a layer of drainage material (see pages 108–109) to the base of the pot.

Choosing Containers

The price, style and colour of a container is a personal choice – these will not have an impact on the plant's growth. However, when it comes to the structural design and size of a container, these factors can affect a plant's performance.

The size of a container is an important consideration. The bigger the container, the more compost it can hold. This reduces the frequency of watering and protects the roots from extremes of heat and cold. However, the trade-off is cost and manoeuvrability. As a guide, use a minimum of a 2 litre pot at least 15 cm (6 in) in diameter for smaller salad leaves and herbs. A 10 litre pot (about the size of a domestic bucket) can support a group of three to five different types of plants. Thirsty plants, such as runner beans, cucumbers and tomatoes, will benefit from a large 15 litre container (the size of a builder's bucket).

Containers with a depth of less than 15 cm (6 in) will subject plant roots to extremes of waterlogging and drying out. If you use them, the plants will need daily attention. New compact plant varieties have reduced the minimum size of pot required, so feel free to experiment, but the sizes above should yield good results.

Traditional flowerpots

The shape of the classic terracotta flowerpot has evolved over the centuries,

Terracotta flowerpots come in a variety of shapes, sizes and styles, glazed and unglazed. Choose ones in a similar style, or mix and match them.

so it now has enough depth for drainage, but is wide enough at the top for plants to thrive. Over time, unglazed terracotta will take on a patina that is often considered more attractive than new pots; this is due to its porous nature. Glazed pots have less porous sides, so they are better at holding water, but the glazing can crack in winter. See the 'Material checklist', opposite, for other material choices.

It pays to think ahead when it comes to finding planting containers. You can often find bargains after the growing season. For a less expensive option, consider buckets, storage boxes or crates; these can be recycled options as long as you are sure they have not been used to store harmful chemicials.

Although flowerpots sold for interior use often look pretty, be wary of using them outdoors. They have no drainage holes and heavy rain can saturate small pots of herbs and kill the roots within a few days. It may be possible to make drainage holes, but these pots usually do not wear well outdoors; they can become disfigured, even fall apart, within months.

Window boxes

Rectangular planters near a window are a popular option. Wood is the most versatile material for a window box, and it can be custom made to fit your window, then painted, stained or varnished to your taste. Use a solid liner if you want to change old displays easily, or choose a porous liner to allow for drainage, thereby limiting rot.

Securing the boxes depends on how the window opens and whether there is a windowsill. There are options for all possibilities,

Some plants such as basil dislike water on their leaves; a saucer provides water below the foilage, but don't let the compost get saturated with water.

but it can take time to locate a supplier; an internet search will be useful. Also make sure you can safely reach the plants from the window, or they will be difficult to water.

Other containers

Plastic hanging baskets and window boxes are available with built-in water reservoirs. These are filled up through an easy-to-reach tube. They need watering two to three times less often than a conventional container of a similar size. They are suitable for plants that need a moist compost, such as lettuces and Oriental greens, but not for plants that prefer drier conditions.

Inexpensive growing bags are plastic bags filled with compost that are shaped so you can plant straight into them after making cuts in the plastic. They can be used, with supports, for tomato, cucumber and pepper plants.

Planning ahead

Before you purchase the plants, check that you have any liners, brackets, supports and drainage material, such as crocks, gravel or polystyrene packing peanuts used for shipping items (you will need enough to line 5 cm/2 in at the base of the pot). Plan to complete any jobs – such as painting supports or attaching brackets to walls – before the plant buying and growing season starts.

Grow for it!

Material checklist

- **Fibreglass** Lightweight and frost-resistant; it can be moulded into different faux finishes, including copper and lead, or with motif patterns. Fibreglass pots are expensive but durable.
- **Metal** Inexpensive metal planters often have sharp edges, rust easily, even if painted, and get too hot for the roots. Well-finished, good-quality containers can work well; if you are on a budget, consider buckets or old preserving pots.
- **Plastic** Inexpensive, lightweight and often with a good finished appearance, plastic pots have many useful features such as water reservoirs and drip trays moulded in. Thin plastic does not age well because it can fade, buckle or split.
- **Terracotta** Although widely used for growing plants outdoors, most terracotta flowerpots are only frost-tolerant, not frost-resistant, so glazes flake and crack if left outdoors in winter.
- **Terrazzo** Made of fine marble chips mixed with concrete and polished to a smooth finish, these pots keep the roots cool, but they are expensive and heavy.
- **Wood** Make sure the wood is a rot-resistant type suitable for outdoor use, such as cedar. Glued boxes fall apart; inspect the joints. End-of-season maintenance such as revarnishing or painting may be required to keep them looking attractive.
- **Wicker and rattan** Rustic and lightweight, both materials are good for tabletop displays and hanging baskets. They often come already lined, but these are not durable.

Growing from Seed

Sowing your own seed instead of buying young potted plants is an option, even if you are growing plants in containers instead of directly in the ground. By growing plants from seed, you'll have a greater choice of varieties.

You can raise many annuals from seed, but in a small area you should concentrate on a few subjects or you will have too many plants. Any salad leaves that you want to harvest a little at a time and often is a good choice to grow from seed. One or two seed packets at the start of the season will be all you need. Root crops such as carrots and beetroots do not do well when transplanted, and one seed or plant provides you with only one or a small cluster of roots, so start these from seed. Vigorous crops that grow rapidly such as beans are difficult for commercial nurseries to grow and transport to the consumer, so these are another good option to grow from seed.

Selecting varieties

For a greater choice of varieties, select seeds directly from a mail-order or internet seed supplier early in the year. Some varieties have certain attributes that make them useful for growing in a small space because of their size or appearance, such as a compact yellow courgette, a red-leaved beetroot or a purple-podded pea. New varieties with increased disease resistance are also often available only as seeds.

Sowing indoors

You can start tender vegetables that need high temperatures to germinate and a long growing season, such as tomato, sweetcorn, aubergine and pepper, earlier indoors before

conditions are ideal outdoors. Grow them on a table by a well-lit windowsill in a heated room. Concentrate on hard-to-obtain varieties that will not be available as plants from most nurseries.

Sowing outdoors

All you need for hardy plants is a place with good light that is frost-free, but preferably warmer than the minimum germination temperature. A conservatory is suitable, and so is a cold frame if you have the space. These plants will grow rapidly and you can move them into containers directly outdoors after as few as four weeks; modular trays are ideal. Sow a couple of seeds per cell and if more than one emerges, use scissors to clip all but the strongest seedling later on.

 Grow for it!

Herbs and flowers from seed

Some herbs used in cooking are a good choice for sowing from seed; for example, parsley and coriander are easy to sow and you can harvest them like cut-and-come-again salad leaves. You can grow chervil and dill, which are not often sold as plants, from seed. Basil can be difficult, because it dislikes cold and damp conditions. Unless you can provide 24°C (75°F) for two weeks, buy plants in early summer. Sow edible flowers such as nasturtiums and marigolds in small pots or directly into their final containers.

Choose a site by a bright windowsill, but not one in direct sunlight, to get seeds started indoors. Direct sunlight can scorch the seedlings.

Once the outdoor temperature is warm enough, you can sow many seeds directly into their final containers. Push large seeds such as beans and peas into the compost. Sow smaller seeds such as carrot in patches, then thin them out. Seed packets usually give instructions for sowing in rows, but you can adapt them to sowing in pots by spacing the seeds equal distances apart. Follow packet instructions for how deep to cover the seeds in compost.

Storing seeds

Store seeds in a cool, dry place. A biscuit tin kept indoors will keep seeds fresh for the growing season. Group packets according to the sowing month, and move the seeds you want to sow often forwards after each sowing to remind you to sow again. To save seeds until the next year, reseal the packets and put in an airtight container with a bag of silica gel, then store in the refrigerator.

Germination temperatures

It is tempting to start sowing early, but sowings made too early often fall prey to cold, rot or pests. Wait until the temperature of the compost in the pot is above 5°C (40°F). The calendar month is only a rough guide to the right time to start sowing – the temperature of the compost is a more accurate guide.

A soil thermometer is inexpensive and easy to use. Simply insert it into the compost at the depth the seeds will be sown. Make sure you take readings at the same time first thing in the morning. The temperatures below are the minimum for sowing. A higher temperature is fine for all plants except lettuces, where germination is poor over 70°F (21°C).

- **40°F (5°C)** Broad bean, Oriental greens, lettuces, peas, radish
- **45°F (7°C)** Beetroot, chard, carrot, onion
- **55°F (13°C)** Beans, cucumber, squash, sweetcorn, tomato
- **65°F (18°C)** Aubergine, pepper

Buying Young Plants

Whether you want only a couple of vegetable plants such as one or two peppers or tomatoes, you don't have time to raise plants from seeds or you want to fill some space quickly, buying young potted plants is a handy solution.

Most of the common vegetables and herbs are available in spring as potted plants. The varieties available in garden centres tend to be conventional or are not named. There is a wider choice by mail order if you purchase in winter, but if you are planning a mixed planting, this might not be an option as the plants may not arrive at the same time. Sometimes it is easier to go to the shop to buy a pot, compost and a selection of available plants and get started.

When to buy

In most garden centres young vegetable plants are bought in and displayed throughout the spring. They may be sold as small plugs in polystyrene packs or in small pots. Many tender vegetable plants are put on sale in early spring, yet they cannot be planted outside until late spring. This makes caring for the young plants a lot more work than necessary, because you have to keep them frost-free, and you will probably have to transfer them into larger pots at least once to prevent a disturbance to their growth. However, you will gain little if you wait until the correct time before buying, because the plants should be bought as fresh as possible and top-quality plants soon sell out.

Vegetable plants that produce fruit, such as aubergines, peppers and tomatoes, are often sold later as mature plants.

When buying potted plants – whether they are being sold at a local charity plant sale or a garden centre – always look for healthy leaves.

These are a good choice if you are unsure about the varieties, because you can judge for yourself their final size and shape.

Herbs are sold in small pots from early spring. Because most are hardy, this is a good time to buy instead of waiting until bigger, more expensive plants are on sale. However, if you have nowhere to keep them frost-free, delay buying tender herbs, such as lemon verbena and basil, until after the last expected frost in your area has passed. Put garden fleece, folded over to use at double thickness, over plants at night if there is an unexpected frost. Secure the edges to stop it blowing away. Special covers are available to protect hanging baskets.

Checking the quality

When buying potted plants always buy freshly delivered stock, because plants soon dry out and deteriorate when kept in small packs or pots for several weeks. Look for stocky or bushy plants with healthy green foliage. Avoid straggly or leggy plants that have

When moving a plant into a new pot, support it at the base, near the top of the compost, and set the plant in the new pot at the same level.

been deprived of sufficient light. Also avoid plants with unnatural, discoloured foliage; this is a sign of stress, frost exposure or lack of nutrients. Inspect young growth for aphids; these will spread to other plants.

Open packs of plants delivered by mail order on arrival, and transfer them into larger pots as soon as you can to prevent them becoming pot-bound (when the roots wrap around themselves in the pot), and put them in a bright, frost-free place. If there is a quality issue, let the supplier know immediately rather than wait in hope that the plants will pull through.

 Grow for it!

Hardening off plants

Plants growing indoors need to be introduced to the outside gradually. After the last expected frost in your area has passed, put the plants outside in a sheltered spot for an hour on the first day and bring them back inside, then increase the time over a week. You can plant hardy plants, such as lettuces, peas and onions, outside immediately, unless they were displayed indoors, in which case they need to be hardened off for a week. Keep tender vegetables, such as courgettes, beans and sweetcorn, in a bright, frost-free place, and harden off for ten days before planting out after the last frost date. If planting outside is delayed by more than two weeks, transfer them into larger pots or feed with a diluted fertiliser. You can use a small cold frame, or 'plant house', of glass or plastic with a wood or metal frame to avoid having to move the plants around.

Planting the Containers

By taking a few easy steps to prepare the pots, you will be giving your plants the best start and make them easier to care for later – whether you sow seeds or introduce young potted plants to their final containers.

Container planting usually begins in the spring months. Start with the hardy plants such as perennial herbs, strawberries, beetroot, lettuces, garlic and onions. Save the tender plants, such as aubergines, beans, courgettes, tomatoes and basil, until last. If you have a light, frost-free space, use it to get a head start with crops that need a long growing season, such as sweetcorn.

Make sure the containers and compost are at a comfortable height. If using small pots, work on a bench or table; if you are using large ones, kneeling down instead of bending over is more comfortable. Put hanging planters in buckets while planting to prevent them tipping over.

Liners and drainage

If a container is likely to rot or discolour when in contact with damp compost or if the sides are open – such as a crate or an open mesh basket – you will need to line the container. Use thick plastic, coir matting or hessian. Use a sharp utility knife to make some drainage slits, but do not trim the edges until a few days after planting because the wet compost will pull it down.

Check that the container has enough drainage holes. Use a power drill to make more holes in the base of wooden, plastic, metal or fibreglass planters. Terracotta or glazed pots usually have one central hole. Cover it with a piece of wire mesh or newspaper so the compost won't be washed straight through.

In the days when all pots were made of clay, pieces of broken clay pots were used as drainage material. You can still use broken pieces of clay pots, or 'crocks'.

 Grow for it!

Types of compost

The smaller the pot, the better quality the compost you need. For large containers, the compost quality is less critical. You can use garden soil to supplement more expensive compost, but finish with a layer of fresh compost to suppress any weed seeds.

- Multipurpose compost is convenient and all edibles will do well in it; you can use a fertiliser to provide extra nutrients. All the plantings grown for this book were raised in a loam-free compost. If you bought a compressed type, break it down with your fingers and fluff it up. Coir-based mixes may need sieving to remove long fibres if you are using it in small pots.
- For long-term plantings such as roses, a loam-based compost lasts longer. Loam-based composts are heavy, so for roof gardens or balconies, use clay aggregates or perlite mixes.
- Citrus plants need a lime-free citrus compost with matching fertiliser, usually available online.

Preparing the container before planting

Start by adding a layer of drainage material. You can break up pieces of terracotta pots or china with a hammer; wear gloves and goggles. Alternatively, use small stones or gravel, polystyrene packing peanuts or even pieces of polystyrene from bedding packs. You can put the drainage material into mesh bags (such as those used for selling onions) so it is easy to remove at the end of the season. Drainage material can be kept in pots year after year.

In small pots the compost needs to hold moisture without becoming waterlogged; add preferably organic, water-retaining granules to help retain the moisture without the soil getting saturated. For any size container, half-fill it with the compost.

Sowing seeds and preparing potted plants

You can sow seeds into containers of moist compost. Most packets have instructions on seed depth and spacing but they assume you will be sowing in rows in the ground. Sow in rows in square containers, with 10 cm (4 in) between rows, and harvest younger. In round pots, scatter the seeds over the surface thinly, lightly cover with compost and thin out later as they grow.

Water plants well before transplanting them, and make sure they are hardened off first (see page 107) if the container is going outside immediately. However, you can plant hanging baskets and pouches earlier, when the plants are smaller, and keep them in a bright and frost-free place.

Moving a plant into a larger pot

1 Remove a plant from its original pot by tapping the side of the pot to loosen the compost and then carefully sliding the pot from the roots, making sure the other hand is supporting the plant at its base.

2 Position the plant in the new container at the same level that it was in its original pot. Pack in the compost around it and firm in gently, pushing the compost into corners if there are any; if you leave air gaps, the roots will dry out.

3 Once the plant is in, fill in around it and the edge of the pot with more compost. Leave a 2.5 cm (1 in) gap between the surface of the compost and the rim; this allows the water to seep down instead of running off the top.

Caring for Your Crops

Once the container plantings have been assembled, the plants should grow rapidly and be ready for harvesting within weeks. There are just a couple of things to bear in mind to get the best results.

When growing plants in pots, keeping the compost consistently moist but not waterlogged is key. This is not as obvious as it sounds; for example, during rainy periods, pots close to the house can remain dry or, if there are big leaves, the water may run off and never reach the roots. Conversely, heavy rain can saturate the compost and starve the roots of air – that is why drainage holes and materials are so important. If you use a saucer under the pot, make sure it doesn't sit full of water for days at a time. When a compost is extremely dry, it can be difficult to re-wet because the water runs along the side of the pot. In such cases, submerge small pots in clean water with one or two drops of washing-up liquid until

Slugs and snails avoid crossing over copper as it gives them small electric shocks, so apply sticky-backed copper tape around a pot to protect the plants.

they stop bubbling, then drain. Reduce the need for watering by moving plants into the next pot size up, so there is a greater volume of compost, or move pots to a cooler, shadier spot. You will need to arrange some care, or a watering system, for your plants when you go away (see 'Holiday watering', page 101).

Fertilising plants

Growing plants will use up the nutrients in the compost within about four weeks, even less if the pots are small or the container is densely planted. To make sure the plants put on healthy growth and produce a crop, you may need to supply a fertiliser. One option is to mix in slow-release fertiliser granules that last the growing season into the compost when the pots are planted up, which saves time. Another option is to supply the fertiliser as a liquid feed, which is provided when watering through the season. Liquid feeding provides nutrients that are taken up by the plant quickly. Typically, either a concentrated liquid or granules are diluted with water in a watering can and then watered on weekly or fortnightly.

A balanced liquid feed has equal amounts of the main nutrients. Crops to prioritise for balanced feeds are: beetroot, Oriental greens and spinach. Then comes celery, beans, garlic, kale, lettuces and cut-and-come-again salads, onions, potatoes and shallots. If you can invest in another fertiliser, a more common option for leafy crops is to feed with a fertiliser containing more nitrogen. A tomato fertiliser has a higher ratio of potash to encourage fruit production and often contains trace elements from ingredients such as seaweed extract. The following fruiting crops have a low nitrogen requirement but are fed diluted tomato feed to provide potash for fruiting: aubergines, courgettes, cucumbers, peppers and tomatoes. Carrots, sweetcorn, fennel, peas, radishes and most Mediterranean herbs do better without added fertiliser.

Because the aim is to eat the plants you are growing, consider using organic fertilisers. Whichever type of fertiliser you decide to use, always follow the packet instructions carefully for applying it.

Pests

Slugs and snails are a main concern, and attacks are worse during mild, damp conditions. Young leafy crops are the most vulnerable early on, and fruiting vegetables are attacked in summer and autumn. Organic slug pellets are a popular control method because they are inexpensive and easy to apply. Moving containers off the ground, on to tables, for example, can help make it difficult for the slugs and snails to find them.

Grow for it!

Making the most of the space

Unlike purely ornamental container plants, which can flower until the first autumn frost, you may need to fill gaps from early summer onwards after harvesting crops. Have a selection of reserves in small pots ready to go in, and keep them somewhere unobtrusive but where you will remember to water them.

If you have little space, how about a window box on the shed or even a garage or a table with shelves outside the back door? After harvesting an early summer crop, such as shallots, early potatoes or lettuces, follow them with tender vegetables started off in indoor pots, such as courgettes, tomatoes, sweetcorn or dwarf beans. Later in the summer, plant Oriental greens outside to replace those harvested in early summer.

Healthy, tasty edibles – such as these mizuna leaves – will be the result if you care for your plants as they grow.

Aphids can suck the sap from plants, which are then weakened, and the yield can be affected. Some aphids spread viruses from one plant to another; for example, mosaic virus can be introduced into a courgette plant, which will wither and die. A well-aimed strong jet of water can knock off aphids, but only try this on mature, well-rooted plants. Early in the year, garden fleece will protect plants from aphids, as well as carrot fly and cabbage white butterflies. Late in the summer use a fine mesh cover. Weigh down the edges so pests cannot get in. You can wash and reuse the covers, but check them for holes before using them again.

Diseases

Soil diseases are rare in container growing, assuming you start with compost that is fresh or has been used only once for a different crop. Grey mould (*Botrytis*) can be a problem, so use clean water and moisten the compost, not the leaves, flowers or fruit. Remove any dead or rotting plant remains promptly to prevent the disease spreading. Blight is spread by raindrops, so it can be a problem in tomatoes and potatoes; bringing them under cover when there is a forecast of blight (check online) can help.

What to Grow

Here's a hand-picked selection of vegetables that will provide the best results in small spaces. All are annuals, which means they will grow, produce a crop and die off in just one growing season. They need light, shelter, moisture and nutrients, plus regular care from you, to keep them growing healthily, so check the individual entries to see what your favourites will need. Salad leaves and other leafy vegetables are quick to grow, but root vegetables such as carrots and fruiting vegetables such as tomatoes take longer – choose a mixture of leafy, root and fruiting crops to spread the harvest over a longer time.

Dwarf Beans

By far the most hassle-free bean for window boxes, pouches or hanging baskets, dwarf beans are neat in habit yet prolific, so you don't even need a garden to grow beans.

Getting started

What to plant Seeds or plants
Site Sunny
When Plant outside in spring after the last frost; sow little and often
Container size 4 plants in a 10 litre container
Spacing 13–15 cm (5–6 in)

Dwarf beans are now also known as bush beans, but whatever you call them, growing these beans in containers raised off the ground makes them easier to pick than those grown in a garden, and the pods will be a higher quality because they will be lifted away from soil and slugs. Dwarf bean varieties with purple and yellow pods will also provide extra ornamental value. The green varieties also have their place, because a mixture of yellow and green beans are attractive on the plate. (Purple pods turn to green when cooked.)

Filet beans, which are also called French beans, have long, thin pods that crop extra quickly, and you can start picking them when the pods reach 10 cm (4 in) long. The purple types, such as 'Royal Burgundy' or 'Purple Teepee', hold their pods well above their foliage for easier picking.

Round-pod types are plumper and picked when the pods are 15 cm (6 in) long; 'Blue Lake' and 'Tendercrop' are typical. For yellow pods, look for a wax bean such as 'Pencil Pod Wax'. Shelling beans are varieties with larger seeds. They can be picked as normal dwarf beans but are best picked later as green beans or flageolets, or as mature pods when the bigger seeds can be shelled as haricots.

Planting

You can buy potted plants, but for the greatest choice of ornamental varieties buy seeds from catalogues or an internet source, and start them in small pots indoors, sowing in batches from March to

Keeping dwarf beans raised off the ground will mean less backaches when it comes to picking them – and the beans won't pick up soil.

May. The plants are frost-tender but, being small, they fit neatly under a crop cover. To maintain a continuing supply of fresh beans, make additional sowings until early July directly into the compost.

Broad beans

Because broad beans are hardier than dwarf or climbing beans and crop early, they are worth considering in areas with a mild winter; however, they are not the neatest or the most productive of beans for containers. Look for dwarf varieties such as 'The Sutton', which grows to 60 cm (2 ft) and needs only minimum support. The early flowers will also attract beneficial insects.

Seeds normally germinate at 10°C (50°F), producing an early crop around June in an open, sunny site with shelter from strong winds. Simply push four seeds 3.75 cm (1½ in) deep into a 10 litre pot of compost in midspring. If it is dry when the flowers form, water well once a week to improve the quality of the final crop. When the plants are in full flower, pinch out the top 10 cm (4 in) of each plant. This encourages the pods to form and, because this is where aphids gather, it also gets rid of the pests. You can remove the plants after harvesting and replace them with late-flowering perennials such as penstemons.

Pick the lower pods first as they mature. For shelling, pick the pods when the seeds inside are just showing and are still soft. You can also pick young, tender pods and eat them whole. Note that some people of African, Mediterranean, or South-East Asian descent have an allergic reaction to raw broad beans and should avoid eating them.

The seeds germinate best at 13°C (55°F); sow one seed per 7.5 cm (3 in) pot. Sow a few extra pots to allow for any failures. Once their roots have almost filled the pot, harden them off (see page 107) and plant them outside into their final container. To grow as a single planting, allow four plants to a 30 cm (12 in) diameter pot.

Care

When the first flowers start to form, keep the compost moist to increase the harvest. If you grow them in an exposed site, the plants may need a little support to stop them flopping over. Use small pea sticks to support them or string tied around garden canes pushed into the pot.

Harvesting

Once the pods start to form, pick all the 10–15 cm (4–6 in) long pods. If you let the seeds start to mature in unpicked pods, flowering will begin to decline. To prolong the harvest pick any surplus pods and freeze those you cannot eat. The plants will provide a crop for about three weeks.

To pick a bean, snap each bean off, using your finger and thumb, or snip it off with a pair of scissors. Avoid pulling them off because this will dislodge the plant and damage the roots. Fresh beans are one of the best crops to grow for freezing – simply blanch and freeze (see 'Freezing', page 117). Leave shelling beans to dry and ripen naturally. Cover the plants during wet spells or bring them indoors to dry in a sunny, airy room. Eventually, the pods will be dry and brittle, and then you can easily separate the seeds and store them in airtight jars.

When the beans are long enough for harvesting, you may need to pick them as often as every other day when the plants are at their peak.

Climbing Beans

Not only are climbing beans attractive annual climbers with colourful flowers, they also make excellent use of vertical space and produce large quantities of beans.

Getting started

What to plant Seeds or plants
Site Sunny or partial shade, sheltered from wind
When Plant outside in spring after the last frost
Container size 2 or 3 plants in a 10 litre pot
Spacing 15 cm (6 in) apart

Plant two seeds together to make sure you have a plant. If both seeds happen to germinate, you can allow them both to grow together.

Climbing beans were grown as ornamentals before it was discovered you could eat the beans. They provide a pretty summer screen, which is useful in an urban or small garden for privacy, but position them where they will not cast shadows over other crops. There are two types, runner beans and French beans. French beans give a better crop earlier in the season, while runner beans crop better later on. French beans do not rely on insects to pollinate the flowers.

For colourful flowers, choose bicolours, such as the red and white 'St George'. For red flowers, consider 'Wisley Magic'; try 'Celebration' for salmon pink flowers. 'Moonlight' has white flowers and is a cross between a runner bean and a French bean – it is self-pollinating with a runner bean flavour. French beans are available with green pods such as 'Blue Lake' but also with yellow pods ('Neckargold') and purple pods ('Violet Podded Stringless').

Compact climbing varieties are handy for containers where a tall support is not feasible. They are still taller than dwarf beans, so they will need some support from canes (pea sticks are handy); 'Hestia' has attractive red and white bicolour flowers.

Planting

You will need a large tub or half barrel with bamboo canes or a long, rectangular planter with a trellis panel or a similar built-in support. An alternative is to grow the beans in a long, rectangular trough against a sunny wall covered with netting. The canes need to be 1.8–2.4m (6–8 ft) tall in a 60–90 cm (2–3 ft) diameter container. Tie the top ends together – use garden string

Shelling and drying

Shelling beans are a halfway house between fresh and dry beans. They are left in the pod to swell, then shelled and used before they dry. Grow beans for drying in the warmest spot, so they can dry as much as possible on the plant. If rain is forecast, either cut the dried stems and bring them inside, or untie the beans, lay them down on a sheet of plastic and put a rainproof cover over them. When they are completely dried, remove the pods and shake out the dried beans. Remove any damaged ones and store the rest in airtight jars. You can store the beans along with clean pods, or shell them and store in an airtight container. Soak overnight before cooking.

Freezing

At their peak of cropping, even a few dwarf bean or climbing bean plants can produce more beans than you can eat fresh. The best way to preserve fresh beans is to freeze them. Choose the best-quality beans and aim to freeze the beans the same day you pick them. Bring a large saucepan of water to the boil and prepare a bowl of cold, iced water. Pick the beans, clean, top and tail them and slice, if they are large. Place them in a steamer basket, plunge it into boiling water for 2–3 minutes, then plunge it into the iced water for 2–3 minutes and drain. Divide the beans into meal-size portions and put into freezer bags or containers. Label and date them; use within four to six months.

or wire, or make an attractive feature by being creative with the material and method you use to secure the canes. To grow climbing beans up a fence, trellis, arch or pergola, use netting to help support them.

Sow two seeds per 13 cm (5 in) pot. Keep the pots at 10–12°C (50–54°F). If both germinate, do not separate them but plant both together. Continue to grow them at a minimum temperature of 7°C (45°F) until they are 15–20 cm (6–8 in) tall.

Gradually harden off young plants (see page 107) to prepare them for planting outside. You can also sow the seeds directly into containers after the danger of late frost has passed. Sow 2 cm (¾ in) deep when the compost is 10°C (50°F).

Sow or plant two or three plants per 10 litre pot. Sow or plant two seeds to each support at 15 cm (6 in) intervals.

Care

In exposed areas, protect young plants from cold winds until they are well established. If the first shoots flop, wind them anticlockwise around the support and tie them in. Eventually, the plants will cling on to the supports by themselves.

Water the compost regularly in dry weather. Give generous soakings to encourage flowering and increase the size of the pods. When the plants reach the top of their supports, pinch out their growing tips; this will encourage the formation of side shoots.

You can protect plants from slugs and snails by wrapping sticky-backed copper tape around the pot. Aphids can build up rapidly in the summer, stunting the plants and reducing the crop. Natural predators such as ladybirds will help keep them under control. If not, you can spray with an insecticide soap; make sure you follow the packet instructions carefully.

Flowers sometimes fail to produce pods. Cool spells may discourage pollinating insects, or high night-time temperatures or drought can cause the embryo beans to abort. Water the compost in hot, dry weather, but do not spray the flowers.

When climbing beans are ready to harvest, pick every bean, even if you cannot eat or freeze them all, to prolong cropping into late summer.

Harvesting

Pick the beans when they are 18 cm (7 in) long. If they grow too large, they will become tough and stringy, and there will be a decrease in the crop. To check, the bean should snap cleanly without any string. Before you go on holiday, pick even the tiniest beans and flowers so you have a continuing crop when you return.

Beetroot

These sweet-tasting roots really earn their keep in a small space. Both the leaves and roots can be eaten, and you can leave them planted in the container until needed.

The flavour of baby beetroot is at its best when the roots are the size of a golf ball.

Getting started

What to plant Seeds
Site Sunny or partial shade; rich compost
When Sow in early spring, in small amounts biweekly for baby beetroot, until midsummer
Container size Any for baby beetroot
Spacing Sow seeds 2.5–5 cm (1–2 in) apart

For baby beetroot, look for quick-maturing varieties such as 'Red Ace', 'Pablo' or 'Detroit Dark Red'. 'Bull's Blood' has bright red foliage; you can use its young leaves in salads (the roots are disappointing). For beetroot to serve as a vegetable, try the golden yellow roots of 'Burpees Golden', or try 'Chioggia' – its rings of red and white will blend to pink when cooked. 'Boltardy' is an old variety that keeps well until needed.

Planting

For quick, even germination, soak seed 'clusters' (beet seeds are not true seeds but a dried fruit with several seeds) in warm water overnight before sowing. Sow two seed clusters in a 7.5 cm (3 in) pot 2.5 cm (1 in) deep. Keep the pots somewhere cool but frost-free. Beetroot will germinate at 10°C (50°F). When the seedlings have their first true leaves, transfer them as a clump to their final container and space the clumps 15 cm (6 in) apart.

Or, if growing as a single planting, sow directly in the final container, placing a seed cluster 5 cm (2 in) apart each way.

For a supply of baby beetroot, sow at regular intervals in spring and summer. If you are growing beetroot for storage, sow once in summer (May–June) and harvest from August or September onwards. Pull every other root as a baby beetroot, and let the remainder grow to full size for winter storage.

Care

Keep the compost evenly moist. Watering, or even heavy rain after a dry spell, will cause the roots to split. Feed with a balanced all-purpose fertiliser fortnightly. Even if insects attack the leaves, the roots will still be edible. Pick off and destroy severely affected leaves.

Harvesting

After the plants have been growing for four weeks, you can pick a few young leaves from each plant to use in salads. Later on, older leaves are a good spinach substitute. Harvest baby beetroot when 2.5 cm (1 in) in diameter. Twist off the leaves but keep the thin tap root intact. (This helps prevent the colour bleeding during cooking.) You can keep beetroot in the ground until the first frost, when the ground freezes. Pull beetroot when 5 cm (2 in) in diameter. Rinse beetroot in water to clean them before cooking them in their skins, then rub the skins off. Store beetroot in a refrigerator for up to three weeks in a plastic bag. The leaves will stay fresh for a week.

Pak Choi & Oriental Greens

In the right conditions, pak choi and other Oriental greens are attractive and quick crops that provide salad leaves, cooked greens and stir-fry ingredients, all from the same container.

Getting started

What to plant Seeds
Site Cool partial shade; rich, moist compost
When Early spring or late summer
Container size Any
Spacing 2.5 cm (1 in) apart and thin to 20 cm (8 in)

In the category of Oriental greens, seed companies list many types of fast-growing edible leaves, often combined in a mix with pak choi, recognisable by its head of white stems with bright green or red-purple, broad leaves. Mizuna has deeply serrated leaves, while mibuna has more

The fleshy white stems of mature pak choi add crunch to a salad. The leaves are ideal in stir-fries.

rounded leaves. When young, they have a mild mustard taste, which develops into a stronger, rougher flavour. Both mature in only 40 days. Mustards are even hotter in flavour and the red-purple varieties are attractive plants.

Planting

Oriental greens are a good crop to plant after lettuces, spinach or rocket, because you can sow them in late summer for an autumn crop. Pak choi grows best in cool conditions in a moist compost. In cool areas, sow in early spring and repeat in July for an autumn crop. In mild or warm regions, sow in late summer. In cold areas, sow the seeds in modular trays four weeks before the last frost, then harden off (see page 107) before moving outside. Sow a seed 1 cm (½ in) deep every 2.5 cm (1 in) and thin out in stages by removing every other plant for baby leaves and allow the rest to grow bigger. Or for only mature plants, sow the seeds 20 cm (8 in) apart or according to the packet instructions; varieties do vary.

The pointy leaves of the fast-growing mizuna are either green, as above, or a red-purple colour.

Care

These plants grow rapidly, so most of the care is aimed at keeping the compost moist to prevent the plant producing flowers (bolting) instead of leaves. Feed with a balanced all-purpose fertiliser every two weeks. Many pests such as flea beetle are attracted to these plants, so protect them with a fine mesh cover.

Harvesting

Pick young leaves for salad greens or let the plants reach full size. Cut the plant to 2.5 cm (1 in) above soil level and let the stump regrow a second flush of leaves.

Carrots

Sweet and crunchy baby carrots are ideal for containers, and their feathery foliage is an attractive feature that works well with patio flowers.

Regular, full-size carrots need a deep container and are slower growing, but they are a better choice if you want to store carrots for the winter.

Getting started

What to plant Seeds or seed tape
Site Sun; sandy compost
When April, then every 6–8 weeks until August
Container size At least 30 cm (12 in) deep
Spacing Sow seeds 2.5 cm (1 in) apart; thin to 2.5 cm (1 in)

Early carrot varieties produce a usable root quickly, so they are the best types to sow in spring for the earliest crop of carrots. You can also sow them regularly throughout the season for a succession of baby carrots or leave them to mature for winter use. Any 'Amsterdam' type will quickly produce finger size roots that children love to eat raw. 'Nantes' carrots, with 15 cm (6 in) long roots, are easy to prepare for cooking, as are the 'Chantenay' types, which form short, broad roots. Round types such as 'Parmex' are a good choice for shallow containers.

Planting

Scatter the seeds thinly – aim for a seed every 2.5 cm (1 in) – on moist compost.

Cover with a 5–10 mm (¼–½ in) layer of compost. Use seed tape, where the seeds are sandwiched between long paper strips, if handling the tiny seeds is awkward. Carrot seeds are slow to germinate, but they will grow once the temperature reaches 5°C (41°F). When the seedlings are big enough to handle, gently pull out extra seedlings so plants are about 2.5 cm (1 in) apart.

Care

Carrots growing in containers need regular watering in dry spells to keep the compost moist. Sow an early variety every six to eight weeks for a continuing supply of baby carrots. Pull out early sowings before they get too big.

Carrot fly grubs can tunnel into the roots and ruin the crop. The adult flies usually fly close to the ground in their quest for carrots, so lifting a container 75 cm (2½ ft) off the ground or using a fine mesh will help keep the flies from reaching the plants. Because the flies are attracted to the smell of pulled carrots, thin and harvest carrots in the evening, when the flies are not active.

Harvesting

If the roots do not slide out when you pull the bottom of the leaves gently, use a hand fork to ease them out. To store for a few days, cut off the leaves or the roots will shrivel.

Storing carrots in winter

In early summer, make one sowing of a full-size carrot variety such as 'Resistafly' or 'Purple Haze'. Thin out the carrots to 5–7.5 cm (2–3 in) between plants. In the autumn, lift the roots. To store carrots, layer them in single rows between slightly moist sand in wooden boxes and keep them in a cool, dark place such as a shed.

Cucumbers

Imagine picking a fresh cucumber every day throughout the summer from one or two plants growing in containers near your kitchen door.

Getting started

What to plant Seed or plants
Site Warm, full sun, in well-drained compost
When Plant outside in late spring after the last frost
Container size 10 litre container for modern bush types; at least 15 litre container for vine types
Spacing 30–45 cm (12–18 in) apart

The modern bush varieties have a compact habit ideal for containers, but you can grow even rampant vine types in a large pot or rectangular planter with a trellis for support. 'Bash Champion' and 'Fanfare' are compact bush plants that produce plenty of fruit. Good 'mini cue' varieties include 'Cucino' and 'Green Fingers' with 10 cm (4 in) long fruit ideal for packing into children's lunch boxes.

Planting

In warm areas, insert the seeds into the compost once the soil temperature is 18°C (65°F). In cool areas, start off seeds in individual pots indoors at a temperature of 21°C (70°F). After there is no more danger of frost, harden off the plants gradually (see page 107) before moving them outside into their final pots. Pile the compost into a slight mound in a pot before planting a cucumber; this prevents the plant rotting in water.

Care

After first planted outside, keep watering to a minimum. Make sure the pots have

Water cucumber plants only in the morning to avoid wet soil overnight because plants are prone to rot.

Once the cucumbers form, make sure you regularly pick them, at least twice a week, to help keep the plants producing more cucumbers.

adequate drainage. Once the plants are established, water regularly or install an automatic-drip irrigation system. About six weeks after planting, feed with a tomato fertiliser to promote the development of cucumbers. Keep an eye out for powdery mildew, and remove and destroy any affected leaves.

Harvesting

Pick slicing cucumbers when 15–20 cm (6–8 in) long, usually every other day. 'Mini cue' varieties are ready when 7.5–10 cm (3–4 in) long.

Aubergines

With their large, soft leaves, purple flowers, and eye-catching crop, aubergines are ornamental container plants suitable for any sunny patio.

Getting started

What to plant Seeds or plants
Site Warm, full sun and shelter
When Plant outside in late spring after the last frost
Container size At least 30 cm (12 in) in diameter
Spacing 1 plant per pot

A top-heavy aubergine plant needs a heavy ceramic or terracotta pot to prevent it toppling over. It is best to grow only one aubergine plant per pot because it needs all the sun possible, and it needs support. However, you can add a quick crop of rocket or herbs before the plant starts to produce flowers.

Collecting aubergine seeds

If you grow only one variety of a non F1 aubergine (check the seed packet), it's possible to collect seeds by allowing one or two of the fruit to grow until fully mature, past their edible stage. Remove the seeds, leave to dry and store in a cool, dark place in an airtight container for up to four years.

Aubergines come in many sizes, shapes and colours. The small or egg-shaped ones are the easiest to manage in flowerpots because the weight of long fruit can cause the container to overturn and be easily damaged. Pretty varieties include 'Calliope', 'Listada de Gandia' and 'Pinstripe', all with white and purple striped fruit. For single colours of purple to black fruits, look for 'Amethyst', 'Ophelia' or 'Pot Black'. The older variety 'Moneymaker', with longer purple fruit, is still worth growing – its dark stems are attractive and it fruits early.

Planting

Seeds need to be started early in the year in warm conditions, so it is easiest to buy potted plants in late spring. However, you can sow seeds in small pots and maintain them at 27°C (80°F). Gradually harden off potted plants (see page 107), waiting until well after the last frost before planting outside – the compost needs to be 21°C (70°F) before planting into it.

As long as you position the plant in a warm, sheltered spot, you will have a wonderful display of aubergines as attractive as any flowers.

Care

Once the plants are well established, water and feed with a tomato fertiliser to keep the plant producing fruit. It is usually necessary to provide support for the plants. Spider mites can turn leaves yellow in hot, dry conditions, but misting the foliage daily can prevent an infestation.

Harvesting

Cut off the first fruit when it reaches half its full size. The flesh will be sweet and tender and, by removing one early, you will encourage more fruit to form. Some varieties have spines on their stems, so harvest the fruit carefully.

Kale

A hardy leafy vegetable with an attractive texture and high in nutrients, young kale leaves can be eaten as salad leaves, and later on, mature leaves make tasty steamed greens.

Getting started

What to plant Seeds or plants
Site Cool partial shade in a rich compost
When Early spring and midsummer to early autumn
Container size Any for salad leaves; 90 cm (3 ft) in diameter for winter vegetable
Spacing Plant 30–45 cm (6–18 in) apart

Once a humble winter green, kale has now been rediscovered as an ornamental salad leaf. There are varieties with red-purple leaves such as 'Redbor' and 'Red Russian', and green varieties such as 'Dwarf Green Curled', as well as Italian heirloom types such as 'Nero di Toscana', which has blue-green strap-like foliage.

Kale thrives in cool areas and is hardy. When growing in containers, however, make sure the roots do not freeze.

Planting

For a few plants to fill a container, start the seeds off in 7.5 cm (3 in) pots. The seeds are large and easy to handle. Sow two seeds per pot (or coir pots to prevent root disturbance). If both seeds germinate, remove the weaker one. (If they are close together, snip it off with scissors.)

Grow the young plants in the pots in a sheltered spot outdoors in a cool but frost-free place. Use a fine mesh to protect them from pests such as flea beetle. Slugs may also damage the young plants. If the leaves start to change colour, the plants may be running out of nutrients. Give them a balanced all-purpose fertiliser, or transplant them into a larger pot. (Don't remove the plants from coir pots; just plant the coir pots into the larger pots.)

Transplant into a larger container or raised bed in midsummer. First water the pot or raised bed well. Make a slight depression and plant into the base. This allows for easier watering in a dry summer, until the plants are established.

For container growing, use a flowerpot that holds at least 6 litres of compost and position it where you can water it frequently. You can grow smaller kale varieties as baby vegetables planted as close as 15 cm

Plant kale in a raised bed or large frost-resistant container for fresh winter greens.

(6 in) apart, but for mature kale, plant them about 45 cm (18 in) apart.

Care

Make sure the compost does not dry out. You can apply fertiliser monthly to encourage rapid growth of young leaves.

Harvesting

Cut leaves as required, but the flavour is better after a frost. Wash thoroughly or soak leaves in salted water for 20 minutes, then rinse to remove insects trapped in the curly leaves. You can allow kale to overwinter and it will produce tasty flower stalks and tender young leaves in spring.

Lettuces

The amount of lettuces you can grow in even small spaces is astonishing and, with some careful timing of the sowings, you can have your own salad bar on tap all summer.

Getting Started

What to plant Seeds, plants
Site Sun or partial shade; partial shade best in summer
When Sow in early spring, then make frequent small sowings every two weeks
Container size 15–20 cm (6–8 in) in diameter for a single lettuce; at least 20–23 cm (8–9 in) in diameter for a mixture
Spacing 12.5–38 cm (5–15 in) apart, depending on variety

Loose-leaf and compact heads of lettuces are perfect for growing in flowerpots, window boxes and other containers. They need little care, other than regular watering. By growing your own lettuces from seed, you will have a greater choice of varieties than what is available at supermarkets. As well as green, you can grow red or bronze-leaved lettuces, and many are speckled or streaked with colour. The variations of texture and leaf shape add to their appeal, with frills, crinkles, pointed and lobe-shaped leaves all adding interest to mixed plantings – and you will have a regular harvest of leaves ready for picking.

Firm heads and loose leaves

Lettuce varieties change frequently, so start by choosing the type you want to grow, such as a lettuce that forms a firm head or frilly loose leaves. Next, look at the varieties available within that category, either in seed catalogues or as young

Young lettuce plants will need room to grow to a larger size, so don't crowd them too closely together.

potted plants. There are several main categories to choose from.

- Loose-leaf lettuce types produce lots of leaves but little head. You can cut the outside leaves as needed and leave the rest of the plant to continue growing and supplying new leaves. There are many easy-to-grow varieties. 'Lollo Rossa' has red-tinted edges; 'Salad Bowl' is a reliable variety; 'Oakleaf' has deeply lobed leaves; and frilly leaved 'Lettony' is attractive in containers.

- Butterhead types have round, loose heads and soft-textured leaves with a buttery flavour. 'Tom Thumb' is the smallest. 'Cassandra' is a modern variety with good resistance to fungal disease, while 'Buttercrunch' is an older reliable lettuce.

- Crispheads, or icebergs, are large plants with crinkled outer leaves and a firm, crisp head. 'Mini Green' is a mini crisphead; 'Blush' is similar but has a pink flush.

- Romaine lettuce has long, pointed leaves with a pale, firm head. They are sweet, crunchy and slow to run to seed. 'Little Gem' is a small lettuce variety suitable for close spacing.

To grow smaller varieties, space them 12.5–15 cm (5–6 in) apart. These are a good choice for growing in pots, window boxes or raised beds. Each plant will make a head about 7.5 cm (3 in) across, which is ideal for a salad for two.

Planting

Sow seeds directly into the final container, start them in small pots or buy young potted plants. Sow two or three seeds together, about 1 cm (½ in) deep, in small pots or into a modular tray. Let the seedlings grow until they have four leaves, then transplant them into their final containers. Spacing varies from 23 cm (9 in) to 38 cm (15 in), depending on the variety, but loose-leaf types can be 12.5 cm (5 in) apart. Lettuce seeds germinate well at low temperatures, but at 21°C (70°F) or higher, germination is erratic. In warm regions, sow only in spring and autumn. In cool areas, keep sowing additional batches at two-week intervals to maintain a constant supply throughout the summer.

Care

A compost rich in organic matter will help retain moisture, and a high-nitrogen fertiliser or balanced all-purpose fertiliser will help produce a supply of leaves. Lettuces in containers escape many of the soil pests, but slugs and snails can still be a nuisance. Go out with a torch after dark to collect and dispose of them. Aphids will attack plants in containers as well as in the vegetable plot, so check the undersides of the leaves occasionally for tiny flies and pick off any affected leaves.

Frilly leaved 'Lollo Rossa' lettuce tinged with bronze makes an attractive feature that can take centre stage in a mixed planting.

Harvest lettuce leaves in the early morning, when the leaves are fresh and filled with moisture. As the day progresses they lose moisture and will be limp.

Harvesting

Each sowing of lettuces can provide baby leaves, more mature single leaves and whole heads of lettuces. You can cut loose leaves from the outer edges with a pair of scissors as needed and use them straight away. Whole heads of butterheads and crispheads will keep for a week in the refrigerator. To check that a head of lettuce is ready, lay the back of your hand on top and press gently – it should feel firm. Use a sharp knife to cut off at the base of the plant.

Mesclun Mixes & Salad Leaves

Grow a tasty mixture of salad leaves and herbs, so that you can pick the young leaves for a regular supply of fresh leaves to add to salads.

Getting started

What to plant Seeds
Site Sun or partial shade
When Spring; then small sowings every two weeks until August
Container size 30 cm (12 in) in diameter
Spacing Sow seeds 1–2.5 cm (½–1 in) apart

Growing leafy salad varieties in different pots makes it easier for you to control the mixture of leaves that ends up on your plate.

You can grow almost any edible leaf in a container and harvest it when young, using the increasingly popular 'cut-and-come-again' technique. This involves cutting the leaves to about 2.5 cm (1 in) above soil level, then leaving the stumps for the plants to regrow. The method is ideal for getting lots of salad leaves out of a window box, patio container or small raised bed.

A good place to start is to try seed mixture packets of edible leaves, often labelled as 'Saladini' or 'Mesclun', which usually include lettuces, endive and chicory plus other species. Or choose your favourite salad leaves and make up a combination yourself, either as a mixture or on its own.

Homemade mesclun mixtures

To create your own mixture, start with a lettuce, such as 'Little Gem', 'Green Salad Bowl' or 'Frisby', to add bulk to a salad. Then add your favourite plants, which may include some of the following.

- Rocket has a distinct peppery, nutty flavour and attractively cut leaves; the plants go to seed quickly, especially in hot weather. Make small sowings every few weeks and pick frequently.

- Spinach lends a mild, buttery taste to the mixture; grow it in spring or autumn, as plants tend to bolt in midsummer.

- Lamb's lettuce (also referred to as mâche or corn salad) is slow growing, so it can be swamped by other species; however, it is a hardy type. Lamb's lettuce has a mild, juicy and crunchy flavour.

- Oriental greens (see page 119) such as pak choi and mizuna have a mild peppery flavour when young. The Asian mustards have a hotter flavour.

- Chicory and curly endive add bitter notes – just grow a small amount and pick young.

- To add colour, try kale (see page 123), which has a subtle cabbage flavour. You

Watercress

You might think you need a stream to grow watercress, however, you can grow it easily in a container as long as you place it in partial shade and where you can water it easily. Sow the seeds thinly and cover with 1 cm (½ in) of compost. Water regularly to keep the compost moist. Pick the leaves often to prevent the plants running to seed. Growth may slow down during hot periods but will often restart later. Alternatively, you can try land cress, which will tolerate a drier compost and cold weather. Pick the leaves young before the plants start to flower.

can also add young beetroot leaves (see page 118) or red chard (see page 137).

■ You can grow many herbs that you grow from seeds as cut-and-come-again crops such as coriander, basil and parsley.

Planting

Sow small 10–15 cm (4–6 in) patches of individual ingredients. Or, if you opt for a mixture, sow thinly in bands 10 cm (4 in) wide or scatter in patches. Leave 1–2.5 cm (½–1 in) between seedlings.

To grow mesclun in a flowerpot, choose one with a diameter of at least 30 cm (12 in). Scatter the seeds thinly and cover with 1 cm (½ in) of compost.

To get a head start in spring, the first batch of mesclun in containers can be started off under a cloche. Start the seeds in small pots or modular trays on a windowsill for planting outside when conditions are more favourable. Outside, sow in containers and cover them with cloches. You will need a site in full sun for early sowings, but move the containers to a semishaded site in midsummer to produce a better quality harvest.

Sow small amounts at two-week intervals, or wait until one sowing has germinated or reached a certain stage before sowing the next batch. This should help spread them out over the season.

Care

Water the compost regularly to keep the seedlings strong; too little water can slow down their growth. Watch out for slugs, snails and aphids. Apply a high-nitrogen or balanced all-purpose fertiliser to make sure leaves continue to grow after cutting.

Harvesting

Cut small quantities of leaves, either as whole young plants or as individual leaves, over a couple of weeks. Aim to have another batch coming into production as soon as the previous one is exhausted.

At first, use scissors to cut immature plants or individual leaves as required. Choose the larger leaves from the outside of the plants, leaving small and young

Plant a mixture of salad leaves with different leaf shapes, sizes and textures to create an attractive planting, but make sure the plants don't overcrowd their neighbours.

leaves in the centre to continue growing. Later on, when the leaves are about 10 cm (4 in) long, cut the whole plants, leaving a 2.5 cm (1 in) stump to regrow in the cut-and-come-again fashion. You should get at least two harvests, and possibly up to four, from a sowing. For really fresh salad leaves, pick the leaves at the last minute, wash thoroughly and spin dry.

Peas

Fresh, sweet peas – whether you eat them whole, pod and all, or shell them – are a real summer treat that is possible whatever growing space you have.

Getting started

What to plant Seeds, potted plants
Site Sunny
When Sow in spring where winters are mild, then again in autumn
Container size 30 cm (12 in) in diameter, to hold 16–24 seeds
Spacing Sow seeds 2.5 cm (1 in) apart

You can grow tall climbing peas in pots with wigwams or in large, rectangular planters with a trellis or netting attached to a nearby fence or wall. Or plant a bush variety into a

Make a wigwam in a large planter, using tall bamboo canes secured by twine, for vining peas to climb up.

pot or hanging basket. Tall varieties usually have a longer harvesting period than the shorter varieties from a single sowing. Make several sowings of a short variety every ten days or make a sowing of an early variety as well a regular season variety.

Peas and pods

There are different types of peas to choose from. The thick fleshy pods of snap peas, also called sugar peas, are sweet and crunchy. 'Sugar Snap' grows to 1.8 m (6 ft) but there are varieties under 1 m (3 ft), such as 'Sugar Ann'.

Mangetout have flat pods and should be picked before the peas develop. You can eat them raw in salads or cook them briefly in stir-fries. 'Oregon Sugar Pod' is a typical 75 cm (30 in) high variety, but there are tall heirloom varieties, too.

Shelling garden peas are grown for the peas, not the pods, which have thin walls. Most are vine types. An increasingly popular trend is to eat the tendrils and pea shoots of the plants. There are now varieties such as 'Canoe' and 'Parsley Pea' with more tendrils than leaves.

Planting

Peas are fairly hardy, so sow seeds early outdoors (at 4–10°C/40–50°F). In cold areas, sow indoors in 8 cm (3 in) pots.

In cold areas, start seeds indoors in 7.5 cm (3 in) pots before moving them outdoors to larger pots.

Grow eight plants to a 10 litre container, sowing a few extra seeds to allow for failures. All but the smallest varieties will need support of either pea sticks – use 60 cm (2 ft) long winter prunings from live hardwood shrubs – or netting securely tied to posts. To avoid damaging the plants, put the supports in place in the containers before or shortly after the seedlings emerge. Plant tall varieties 12.5 cm (5 in) apart near their supports.

Care

The plants should cling to the supports, but you may need to tie them in. If the soil is dry, watering well when the plants are in full flower and the first pods starting to form will increase the yield.

Harvesting

The earliest crop will be ready in late spring to summer. Mangetout should have flat pods 5 cm (2 in) long with immature peas inside. Both the peas and pods should be sweet, and the pods crunchy in snap peas. If either type is left too long, they will be stringy and tough. Shelling peas should have uncrowded, round peas. Go over the plants every day or two, picking all pods that are ready. Leaving pods on the plants for too long will reduce the cropping season.

Peas are truly versatile plants, where the tendrils, pea shoots, peas and even sometimes the pods themselves can be eaten.

Peppers

You can easily train both sweet peppers and chillies into neat, bushy plants that will produce enough ripe peppers to more than pay for a prime site on the patio.

Getting started

What to plant Potted plants
Site Sunny and warm; sheltered
When Plant outside after the last frost
Container size Minimum of 20 cm (8 in) in diameter, but depends on variety
Spacing At least 20 cm (8 in) apart, but depends on variety

Chilli plants are particularly decorative and just one plant should keep even an enthusiastic chilli lover supplied all winter. Sweet peppers are larger plants but they produce fewer fruit, so you will need three plants to supply an average family. It is easiest to start with potted plants because the seeds need starting early in the year at high temperatures. Plants are frost-sensitive, so they need hardening off (see page 107) before moving outside.

Whether you prefer hot chilli or sweet peppers, they come in an amazing array of varieties: from left to right are an ornamental chilli 'Aurora' with upright chillies, a cayenne chilli with chillies that are ideal for drying, a yellow sweet pepper, the sweet pepper 'Sweet Banana' and chilli 'Hungarian Hot Wax'. Whatever type of peppers you grow, harvest them in the same way – use a sharp knife or secateurs to cut the fruit from the plant.

Pepper types

Most peppers and chillies do well in pots, but look for early ripening varieties. If growing sweet bell peppers, consider 'Redskin', an early-cropping type, or 'Magno', which produces lots of orange peppers. Besides the typical blocky bell pepper shape, there are other types of sweet peppers, classified by their shape. 'Corno di Toro' refers to the 'bull's horn' shape of the pepper; it is good roasted. Cherry peppers have small fruit.

Chillies also come in different shapes, but the amount of heat is more important. Habanero and Scotch Bonnet peppers tend to be especially hot. 'Padron' can be picked when the fruit is immature, which is useful in the UK when the weather is not ideal for ripening. 'Basket of Fire' is a prolific variety that is both ornamental and edible.

Planting

As the plants begin to fill their small pots, transfer them into 2 litre pots. When these begin to fill, move the plants into 6 litre pots. When the plants reach 20 cm (8 in) high, pinch out the growing tip with your finger and thumb to encourage the plants to form a bushy habit.

Care

Sweet peppers may need support once the peppers start to swell, but chillies should remain bushy. As the plants flower and the fruit matures you may need to water the plants twice a day on hot days; a lack of moisture when the flowers are forming will cause black rot on the fruit. Feed when the first flowers start to form and again after three weeks with a tomato fertiliser.

Harvesting

Peppers and chillies can be cut off the plants at any stage. Green peppers are less sweet and green chillies less hot than when fully ripe; however, cutting them early will encourage the plant to produce more fruit. Peppers and chillies will keep for up to ten days in the refrigerator.

Drying and freezing

You will probably use up any sweet peppers you harvest, but even a single chilli plant will produce a surplus. In hot weather, you can string up chillies and dry them in the sun before storing; chillies with thin skins dry the best. You can also dry chillies in an oven on its lowest setting for 24 hours or more. Freezing in plastic bags is another alternative.

Potatoes

There's nothing like the taste of your own new potatoes. Growing them in containers is a quick and easy way to start that doesn't require digging or soil preparation.

Potato plants produce a canopy of green foliage and some small flowers, but are otherwise unobtrusive; to make a visual impact, choose the planter carefully.

Getting started

What to plant Certified seed potatoes
Site Sunny or partial shade
When Plant in spring; keep frost-free
Container size Minimum 8 litre pot
Spacing 1 tuber per 8 litre pot

You can grow any potato variety in a large pot, but an early season variety will crop quicker and have a neater appearance. Get certified seed potatoes from a garden supplier; supermarket potatoes may carry diseases or be treated with chemicals to stop them sprouting. As soon as they are purchased, put seed potatoes in a bright, frost-free location such as on a windowsill to produce short sprouts.

The containers need to be moved at least once from their initial frost-free place to their final growing position outside. Containers with handles that can be dragged into place are handy. A 10–15 litre container will hold enough compost for two to three tubers, and three containers of this size will be sufficient. Terracotta pots are attractive but budget alternatives include recycled plastic pots used to sell trees, or large planters or buckets. Potato planting bags are another option.

Planting

Three weeks before the last frost date for your area (March–April), half-fill your container with a rich compost and bury sprouted tubers in the compost. As the tops grow, keep covering them with layers of compost until you reach the top of the containers. Potato foliage is frost-sensitive, so wait until there is no danger of frost before moving the containers outside.

Care

If a late frost is likely, cover the potatoes with a double layer of garden fleece overnight or move them under cover. Keep the compost moist; if too dry, the tubers will not form, but if too wet, they will rot. Keep adding compost, but leave a 2.5 cm (1 in) gap at the top of the container for watering. Avoid splashing the foliage. During hot or dry spells, move the containers into partial shade. Feed with a balanced all-purpose fertiliser. Do not grow potatoes next to tomatoes; both are prone to blight.

Harvesting

The tubers are ready to harvest when they are the size of a hen's egg; push your hand gently into the compost and feel for the tubers, or feel for them through a potato bag. To harvest the potatoes, tip out the contents into a wheelbarrow or tub.

Sweet Potatoes

Nutritious sweet potatoes are versatile tubers from vigorous vines. In warm areas (or if you can provide cover), it is possible to grow them in containers.

Getting started

What to plant Pot-grown plants or certified 'slips' (cuttings)
Site Sunny, sheltered from cold winds
When Plant outside in late spring when there is no danger of frost
Container size One plant per 30 litre pot
Spacing 45 cm (18 in) apart

Sweet potatoes can be a rewarding crop, but the vines are sensitive to frost and need 100 days of warmth, day and night, to crop well. However, provide them with a little attention, and you can still grow sweet potatoes in large containers or in raised beds under a sheet mulch with garden fleece on top.

Order cuttings, known as 'slips', or pot-grown young plants from mail order suppliers. 'Beauregard Improved' is a high-yielding variety with orange flesh that is attractive and tasty. 'Georgia Jet' has orange flesh but is harder to grow. You may come across 'O'Henry', a compact variety for containers with cream flesh.

Planting

Slips need to be placed in a jar of water overnight, then potted up in deep pots with the leaves level with the top of the compost. Keep indoors in a warm, well-lit place. Transplant them into larger pots regularly so they don't become root-bound.

Care

The vines spread and root as they grow to form a mat; provide supports and they will climb up and the tubers will be bigger. Pests such as slugs can ruin tubers in raised beds; use organic slug pellets if necessary. Keep the compost moist – but not too wet or the roots will crack – and feed with a tomato fertiliser.

Harvesting

Harvest before the first frost. Turn the tubers out of their pots, or remove the mulch from a raised bed and dig up the tubers. You can store any surplus, but first let the tubers dry in the sun for a day to cure the skin. Wrap each tuber in newspaper and store in a cool but frost-free, dry place.

Leaves sprout from the sweet potato cuttings, and they will eventually form a mat of leaves as the vines spread and climb.

Onions & Shallots

Take a shortcut by purchasing 'sets', and you will have a supply of onions and shallots for storing. Or with just a little more effort you can enjoy a fresh supply of scallions.

In early summer shallots, provide fresh green leaves as a foil to alyssum. In time the tops will dry out and the bulbs will form at the base of the plants.

Getting started

What to plant Sets (immature bulbs)
Site Sunny; moist but well-drained compost
When Plant in spring (March–April) or autumn, depending on variety
Container size Minimum of 45 cm (18 in) in diameter
Spacing 3–4 inches (7.5–10 cm) apart

Onions and shallots are not ornamental crops and they dislike competition from other plants. However, you can tuck them into a corner out of view. An alternative is to grow spring onions (see 'Spring onions' box, right) in small pots, and use them fresh, while still green. Plant onions and shallots in spring and harvest in summer. You can also plant autumn onion sets in October for an early summer harvest.

Planting

Push the onion or shallot sets into the surface of the compost so the tops are just buried, spacing them 7.5–10 cm (3–4 in) apart. If you have leftover sets, you can plant them close together in a small container and cut the young shoots to use as spring onions.

Care

Onions and shallots do not need much watering, and they do not need fertilising, but ensure you do not overcrowd them.

Harvesting

For storing, wait until the tops of the onions or shallots are brown and dry, then move them somewhere protected from rain for the bulbs to ripen and dry off. Trim off the leaves about 2.5 cm (1 in) from the bulb and store the bulbs in a cool, dry place.

Spring onions

You can grow these salad onions in pots at any time and use them fresh (they will keep in the refrigerator for a few days but otherwise do not store well). Scatter the seeds thinly over a 30 cm (12 in) diameter pot filled with compost and cover them with 1 cm (½ in) of compost. Once the seedlings appear, thin the plants so there is a seedling every 1–2.5 cm (½–1 in), using surplus seedlings as you would chives. Keep the compost moist and start to harvest plants as spring onions when they are the thickness of a pencil. Sow a pot every month from March to July.

Radishes

These popular, colourful roots can be small enough to grow almost anywhere, even in shallow containers such as window boxes, or to fill in gaps in larger tubs.

The typical, small spring radishes will be ready for harvesting within weeks – these have more of a peppery bite to their flavour than winter radishes.

Getting started

What to plant Seeds
Site Cool partial shade; rich moist compost
When Early spring to autumn, sow little and often, every two weeks
Container size Any
Spacing Sow seeds sparingly and thin to 2.5 cm (1 in) apart

Not only will radishes grow in a small pot, depending on the type, but they can also be an incredibly quick and easy crop to grow. The real challenge might be in choosing the variety to grow – there are over 200 varieties to choose from in an array of colours including red, white, purple and mauve. The typical, round, red spring varieties such as 'Cherry Belle' and 'Jolly' are the quickest to grow, needing only three to four weeks from sowing, but there are also long-root types such as red 'French Breakfast'. 'Munchen Bier' is one grown for its edible seed pods.

While summer radishes are suitable for the smallest of containers, winter radishes such as mooli are completely different.

These can have roots as long as 20 cm (8 in), so they need deeper pots, and the larger roots need more time to grow – as much as ten weeks.

Planting

Sow summer radishes thinly, about a seed for every 2.5 cm (1 in). You can sow them in March into pots destined for tender crops and harvest before the tender vegetables are planted. Or, after harvesting a crop of peas or other early vegetable, firm down the compost and sow radish seeds into it. Sow small quantities every two weeks.

Winter radishes are different. Sow them once in midsummer and let them grow much larger to store and use in the winter. They can be used raw or cooked.

Care

The plants grow quickly, so there is little care necessary other than keeping the compost moist; there is no need to fertilise them. Flea beetles can attack the leaves, but the roots will still be edible.

Harvesting

Start pulling up the plants when the roots are 2.5 cm (1 in) in diameter; if larger than 5 cm (2 in), they will lose their hot crunch and become strong and pithy. If you forget to harvest the plants, they will flower and run to seed. You can use the pods to add a hot crunch to salads.

Sweetcorn

This plant's tall foliage brings a dramatic touch to containers and, although yields may be small, there's nothing as sweet as freshly picked sweetcorn.

Getting started

What to plant Seeds
Site Full sun; sheltered; sandy or well-drained compost
When Spring; plant outside after there is no danger of frost
Container size Minimum 45 cm (18 in) in diameter and 30 cm (12 in) deep
Spacing Plant 15 cm (6 in) apart

Unusual and fun, sweetcorn looks great in a container, and has plenty of space at the base for low-growing plants. At the moment, you can get only two or three cobs from a large pot, but improvements are on their way. Seed companies are trying to produce varieties that will have high yields in containers, and one such variety is the supersweet 'Mirai 003Y'.

The Native American method for growing sweetcorn, beans and squashes in a mound can be adapted for a large tub with a dwarf bean plant or a compact squash.

There are different types of sweetcorn: heirloom for old-fashioned flavour, sugar-enhanced, super-sweets, which retain their sweetness longer after harvest, and those with extra-tender skins. Be guided by which varieties perform well in your area, to ensure cobs mature before the first frost.

Planting

Plant the seeds into a container of compost after all danger of frost has past. Sweetcorn needs 70–100 days of warm weather from sowing to harvest for ears to fully form. You can start the seeds in small, deep pots, then move the young plants to the final container.

Care

As the plants, grow mound up the compost around them to secure them in the pot. Water is critical as the tassels and ears form. Sweetcorn is pollinated by wind; you can assist by tapping the tassels at the top of the plants so pollen falls on the silks below.

Harvesting

Watch the silks at the end of the ears; when they turn brown and start to dry, the cobs

A tall sweetcorn plant, with a spiky tassel at the top, provides a focal point in a lower planting of orange blossom nasturtiums.

are ready to harvest. To check, peel back the leaves and pierce a kernel; if the juice looks milky, it is ready. Cut off the ear with secateurs; do not pull it or the plant may be dislodged from the pot or damaged. Cook sweetcorn immediately, before the sugars turn to starch. Some types have thin skins so you can eat them raw.

Chard

One of the most colourful and versatile edibles for containers of all sizes, chard is easy to grow and will stay fresh in its container until you are ready to eat the leaves and stems.

Getting started

What to plant Seeds
Site Sun or partial shade
When Sow in spring to summer
Container size Minimum 30 cm (12 in) in diameter
Spacing Sow 5 cm (2 in) apart, then thin

You can eat the baby leaves of chard raw, or let the plants grow to produce mature leaves for cooking as a spinach substitute. The colourful stems of mature plants are

Spinach and leaf beet

Baby spinach works well in a mesclun mix, but to grow plants to serve as a vegetable you need large quantities – its volume decreases dramatically when cooked – and you need to sow every two weeks because the plants bolt to seed quickly. You can try sowing batches in a large container divided into three, sowing every few weeks.

Leaf beet is an easier alternative to spinach. It is high yielding in a small space and will keep producing new leaves if picked over regularly. Leaf beet is a biennial and will not usually bolt until the second year.

also edible – slice them and use for stir-frying, steaming or baking.

For baby leaves, grow chard with other mesclun ingredients. For larger plants, grow as a single subject, because their roots will fill the pot and need plenty of nutrients and water. The most colourful mixture of stems is 'Bright Lights', but you can also get single colour selections.

Planting

The 'seeds' are really a dried fruit cluster with several seeds that will germinate in a clump. You can separate the seedlings or grow them as a clump. A 30 cm (12 in) diameter container will hold three, four or five seed clusters spaced 5 cm (2 in) apart. Cover with 1 cm (½ in) of compost. You can also grow the seeds in modular trays and move them to a final pot.

Care

To grow the plants beyond the baby-leaf stage, keep the compost moist and use a balanced all-purpose fertiliser to keep the

A rainbow of colourful stems and the crinkly texture of the leaves make chard 'Bright Lights' a good candidate for an attractive container planting.

leaves and stems tender. If the plants do not get enough water or nutrients, they will become stringy and tough. Look for slugs and snails hiding among the stems.

Harvesting

Once the plants are growing, pick or cut a few outer leaves and stems from each plant and let the rest continue to grow; or cut the whole plant off at the base, leaving a stump that sometimes regrows. The crinkled leaves can hold a lot of dust, so wash them well in cold water before cooking. The plants may overwinter, then bolt in the spring.

Squashes

Just a few plants will reward you with a plentiful supply of courgettes and other squashes, and your crops will be younger and fresher than those sold in supermarkets, too.

Getting started

What to plant Plants or seeds
Site Sun, shelter
When Plant outside in late spring, when there is no danger of frost
Container size Minimum 30 cm (12 in) in diameter
Spacing About 45–60 cm (18–24 in) apart, depending on the variety

Seed companies are now selecting squash varieties, including courgettes, with a compact growth habit that produces a crop quickly, which are ideal for growing in pots. Look for the yellow squash 'Buckingham' or 'Soleil' and the dark green 'Midnight'. If you

grow only one or two plants, pollination may be poor, which means less fruit. However, 'Parthenon' and 'Cavili' are two varieties that can produce fruit without pollination.

Planting

Squashes are frost-sensitive and dislike wind and cold soil. Give the plants the best start by filling a large pot with compost, mounding it up in the centre and letting it warm in the sun. Harden off young plants (see page 107) and then plant into the mound; the plants may need to be covered with a cloche or garden fleece for a few

Courgette flowers

You can pick and eat courgette flowers – the ones to choose are the large male ones because the females turn into the fruit. The female flowers are recognisable by a small embryonic swelling at their base. Pick the flowers in the morning, when they are completely open, and keep cool. Inspect the flowers for insects before stuffing them or dipping the flowers in batter and frying.

days. Plant two plants in each container, then cut out the weakest one later on.

The large seeds are easy to handle; sow them directly into planting mounds in early summer when the compost is at least 16°C (60°F). Push in three or four seeds, then later pull out the two weakest seedlings. In cold areas, start the seeds in 7.5 cm (3 in) pots a month before the last frost date.

Care

Drip irrigation will help keep the compost moist; avoid getting water on the foliage or stems. Water just enough to keep the compost moist and as the plant grows increase the amount of water. Feeding with a tomato fertiliser will encourage fruit. Watch out for powdery mildew and rotting fruit; remove any affected leaves or fruit promptly. Yellow marks or streaks on the leaves may be a virus. Remove and destroy the plant. However, yellow-fruited varieties often have yellow leaves, but not the streaks or marks.

Harvesting

Start cutting courgettes when they are 15 cm (6 in) long, or for round squashes, 5–7.5 cm (2–3 in) in diameter. Use a knife to cut the fruit from the plant; wear gloves because the plants can be spiny.

Once the plants start to produce a crop, cut the courgettes daily to encourage extra flowers, and therefore more fruit, to form.

More squashes

You can grow other squashes – such as patty pans, with their scalloped-edged flying-saucer shape (below) – in exactly the same way as courgettes, although the plants can be larger. All types of thin-skinned squashes, including courgettes, are prolific croppers, but their soft skins make them unsuitable for long-term storage. 'Summer Ball', which has round, yellow fruit that can be cut young or left to ripen and stored for a short period, is suitable for growing in containers.

Conversely, hard-skinned squashes, which include pumpkins, have an inedible rind, and you can leave them in the sun to ripen and then store the fruit. Of the two, hard-skinned squashes store best, but the plants need at least 1 m² (10 sq ft) per plant, making them impractical for growing in pots. The exception are some acorn types that have a bushy habit, which you could try growing in a large container.

Tomatoes

From compact bushes to sprawling vines, there is no shortage of tomato types – and as long as you can find a sunny site, no matter how small it is, you can grow your own tomatoes.

Getting started

What to plant Plants
Site Full sun, sheltered; rich compost
When Late spring, plant outside after there is no danger of frost
Container size Varies greatly, but at least 20 cm (8 in) in diameter
Spacing Varies, usually one plant per container

There are plenty of good trailing tomato varieties that are the perfect choice for growing in hanging baskets or for tumbling out of tall pots. In addition, plant breeders have been producing ultra-compact varieties such as 'Venus' that will fit in a window box or small 1 litre pot. At the other end of the spectrum there are the vine-like indeterminate types that, if trained (see 'Indeterminate support', above), will continue to provide a crop all season. A

Tomatoes come in an amazing array of sizes, shapes and colours, and your choice may depend on how you want to eat the tomato. From left to right are a compact bush tomato producing medium tomatoes, tumbling tomatoes with tiny fruit, an indeterminate plant that will provide a long supply of larger tomatoes, and one of the varieties that produces elongated tomatoes. Whatever type they are, harvest the tomatoes when fully ripe but before their skins split.

new development for gardeners are 'turbo' tomato plants, which are varieties grafted on to vigorous root stock so the plants grow quicker and stronger with higher yields. Both of these more vigorous plants are best if you want to cook or preserve tomatoes.

Indeterminate support

An indeterminate variety will grow on and on as a single stem. Bring it under control by tying the main stem to a single wooden stake or a metal spiral support with plant ties. Remove any side shoots that emerge where the leaves join the main stem but leave the flower shoots. Remove lower leaves that turn yellow as growth continues.

Instead of sowing seeds, the simplest way to start is to choose two or three different potted plants from a garden centre in late spring. Wait until this time to buy

bushy, healthy green plants. If you buy them too early, you will have to keep them in a light, frost-free place, and they quickly outgrow their pots. However, if you wait too long, the plants may be starved (with purple tinges to foliage) and straggling.

Planting

Plant standard bush, dwarf or patio plants sold in 7.5 cm (3 inch) pots straight into 30–35 cm (12–14 in) diameter hanging baskets, growing bags or other containers with a capacity of at least 11 litres. The ultra-compact ones need an area of

15–20 cm (6–8 in) to themselves, but you can make them part of a mixed basket if there is a large volume of compost to retain moisture. If there is a delay in planting in the final container, pot the plants into the next larger size pot or fertilise them.

Care

Water the plants regularly – an automatic-drip irrigation system is a boon here – and once the plants are established, give them a tomato fertiliser following the packet instructions. If you feed your tomatoes regularly, you could have three times the

crop compared to unfed plants. Provide indeterminate types with support.

Harvesting

Pick tomatoes when the skin reaches its mature colour. This is easy to determine in red, orange and brown varieties, but it is tricky for yellows and whites, so just taste these. Pick before they turn soft or the skin will split as they quickly rot. It is better to pick tomatoes slightly unripe and put them on a sunny windowsill to ripen. Aim to pick all the tomatoes as they ripen because ripe fruit will rot and drop on to the ground.

Basil

Pretty, neat and tasty, a selection of different basil varieties will be perfect for tabletop flowerpots and tidy enough for window boxes, too.

When basil plants are young, take only a few leaves from each plant. You can use these fresh in salads or for topping a pizza straight out of the oven.

Getting started

What to plant Plants or seeds
Site Warm and sunny; they are frost-sensitive
When Sow in mid-spring, then little and often, every two weeks
Container size 15 cm (6 in) in diameter
Spacing 15 cm (6 in) apart

There is a huge range of popular basil varieties that look as good as they taste, including ones with different textures, sizes and foliage colour. Large-leaved basil plants provide leaves in quantity, which is ideal for making pesto. Opt for the classic bush basil or 'Sweet Genovese', which have a strong aroma and are easy to find. Others you might come across are 'Puck', with a neat habit, 'Green Ruffles', which has pale green leaves, and 'Lettuce-leaved'.

Another good ornamental basil is 'Magical Michael', with a neat habit, dark stems and purple flowers. For dark purple foliage, there is 'Purple Ruffles'; the plant is especially colourful when the lilac-pink flowers are out. There are also the Greek and Thai types (see 'Greek or Thai', left).

Greek or Thai

Basil is popular around the world. 'Aristotle' is a small-leaved Greek basil that grows to only 20 cm (8 in) high but can spread to 40 cm (16 in); you can trim it to shape. The flavour is mild but you can use sprigs of whole leaves for a garnish.

For a spicy aroma and aniseed flavour, try Thai basil 'Siam Queen', and use it in stir-fries or Asian dishes. 'Christmas Basil' is a Thai basil with a high oil content (a sign of a great pesto ingredient) but just as important, it is a neat, attractive plant.

Planting

Basil plants are sensitive to frost and cold, damp conditions, so wait to buy plants in early summer. Keep the pots raised up on tabletops, shelves and window boxes for extra warmth.

Alternatively, sow seeds in pots from mid-spring (early April) onwards in a light, warm (at least 18°C/65°F) location such as a heated propagator in a greenhouse or on a kitchen windowsill. Sow three to four seeds in a 7.5 cm (3 in) pot to keep root disturbance to a minimum. Keep the compost on the dry side.

Care

Pinch out the growing tips when the plants are 15 cm (6 in) tall. Protect from slugs and snails. Move them outside once the risk of frost has passed. Pinch out the flower buds to encourage the plant to remain bushy. Continue to keep the compost on the dry side to avoid root rots and diseases.

Harvesting

Use as needed, picking a few leaves from each plant. Before the first frost arrives, when the plants will die, harvest all the leaves; freeze whole in small plastic bags.

Chives

A great little herb for beginners, chives are easy to grow and will come back year after year. Not only are the leaves suitable for eating, but the attractive flowers are edible, too.

Getting started

What to plant Plants or seeds
Site Any sun or partial shade, moist or dry
When Sow seeds in spring
Container size 15 cm (6 in) in diameter
Spacing Plants should be 15 cm (6 in) apart

This pretty, hardy perennial, with its thin, hollow leaves and small mauve flowers, will fit into any space. There is also a white-flowered form, but it is less widely available. Another alternative is the garlic chive (also

The leaves have a mild onion flavour that is suitable for soups, salads and other dishes.

known as Chinese chive); it has a mild garlic flavour, flatter leaves and white flowers.

Planting

Once the temperature reaches 20°C (68°F) in spring, you can sow three to four seeds 2 cm (¾ in) deep in small pots. Thin out the young plants to leave the strongest seedlings. Chives will fit into mixed herb plantings in pots, or you can keep three small pots with chives growing at different harvesting stages. To keep chive plants going year after year, grow them in a loam-based compost.

Care

Chives need little care. The plants self-seed easily, so you may find new seedlings growing near mature plants. The plants are perennials that die down in winter, and they should be cut back to near compost level. When a clump outgrows a pot, you can remove and split it, then replant healthy sections of the clump. Divide the clumps every three years to help prevent

When the flowers appear in early summer, you can use the petals to sprinkle over a salad.

them developing rust, which occurs if they become overcrowded.

Harvesting

Chives have hollow stems that grow from the base, so it is easy to snip them with a pair of scissors. Cut the stems 1 cm (½ in) from the base; if you just snip the tips, they turn brown and look unsightly. When the leaves are green and fresh in summer, harvest enough to freeze for use in winter. Freeze snipped chives on a baking tray, then transfer to a container and return to the freezer.

Coriander

There are coriander varieties that continue to produce plenty of foliage, even when the plants are cut back, so even the smallest pot can supply plenty of fresh leaves.

Getting started

What to plant Seeds
Site Sun or partial shade for leaves; well-drained compost
When Sow in mid-spring (April–May), every four weeks until July
Container size Minimum 15 cm (6 in) in diameter
Spacing 15–20 cm (6–8 in) apart

Choose coriander varieties that are geared to either leaf production or seed production. You can grow some newer varieties such as 'Calypso' as part of a mesclun mix (see pages 126–127) because it is slow to set seed and its growing points are close to the ground. This means that just one sowing can be cut down and will grow again three to five times if the compost is kept moist. Another slow-to-bolt variety is 'Confetti', which has fine feathery leaves that are pretty as a garnish.

For seed production, look for the fast-growing Moroccan coriander. Sow once in May, then harvest the seeds in August.

Planting

Sow seeds directly into their final pots. The seeds are large and easy to handle, so push them 5 mm

The whole coriander plant is edible – the leaves, stems, seeds and even the roots, which are popular in Thai cooking.

(¼ in) down into the compost. Space the seeds 2.5 cm (1 in) apart if you are growing them for their leaves; otherwise, thin the plants to 15–20 cm (6–8 in). You can sow leafy varieties all year round and keep them in a pot on a windowsill.

Care

Plants need little aftercare; just keep the compost moist.

Harvesting

Cut the leaves with a pair of scissors when the plants are 10 cm (4 in) high, cutting back to 2.5–5 cm (1–2 in) from the compost level. If you have a cut-and-come-again variety such as 'Calypso', repeat the harvesting every month or so. Coriander grows quickly, and it matures rapidly beyond being usable in the kitchen, so freeze batches in ice-cube trays in early summer. It is difficult to grow in autumn and winter, so if you want fresh leaves in winter, grow indoors on a windowsill.

Harvest the roots before the plant runs to seed. Use them to flavour soups such as carrot soup and in curries.

Collect the seeds in late summer, when they turn pale brown. To collect them, cut the stalks and put them in a paper bag. The seeds will drop out into the bag after two weeks. When dry, store them in airtight jars in a cool, dark place.

Dill

Its feathery foliage and bright green-yellow flowers make dill an attractive container plant whose leaves and seeds are used in dips, pickles and preserves.

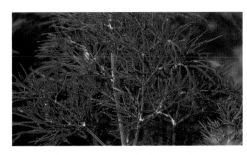

Dill leaves have more flavour before the plant flowers, so pinch out flower stalks if you don't want seeds.

Getting started

What to plant Seed or plants
Site Full sun; well-drained compost
When Sow seeds in late spring (April) and every month until June
Container size Minimum 15 cm (6 in) in diameter
Spacing Thin out seedlings to 10–15 cm (4–6 in) apart

If you want seeds, try 'Mammoth', but most varieties run to seed quickly if their leaves are not harvested. 'Fernleaf' is popular.

Planting

The plants don't like disturbance, so sow the seeds in their final pot or buy potted plants.

Care

At first, let the mix dry out a little between watering; as they mature, keep the compost moist or the plant will flower and set seed.

Harvesting

Cut the leaves once the dill starts growing.

Fennel

A tall herb plant that has green or bronze feathery foliage with an aniseed flavour, fennel can grow in a large, deep tub or a raised bed.

Fennel is an attractive plant to grow with other herbs and flowers in late spring to midsummer.

Getting started

What to plant One plant
Site Sun in fertile compost
When Plant in spring
Container size 60 cm (24 in) in diameter
Spacing 50–60 cm (20–24 in)

A single fennel plant will provide a mass of leaves, so it is suitable for a small site.

Planting

Plant in spring; the plant has a long tap root, so grow it in a large, deep pot. Fennel can reach 1.5 m (5 ft) high in a border, but its growth is less in a container. Be aware: if left to flower, the plant will self-seed. Do not plant near dill to prevent cross-pollination.

Care

If you make sure the tap root has room to grow and keep the compost moist, the plant will thrive. Fennel dies back in winter.

Harvesting

Cut the foliage as required; the stems and flowers can be added to pickles or salads.

Edible Flowers

Enjoy the beauty of edible flowers while they are growing alongside vegetables and salad mixes in containers, then pick a few to add colour to home-grown salads.

Getting started

What to plant Seeds or plants
Site Sun or partial shade
When Sow seeds in early spring or buy potted plants in late spring to early summer
Container size 30 cm (12 in) in diameter
Spacing 15 cm (6 in) apart

If you plan to add flower petals to food, besides making sure they are insect free, use only flowers that have not been sprayed with chemicals. To be sure of what you are eating, either buy organically grown plants or raise your own plants from seed.

Planting

Depending on the flowers, add them to a group planting with other plants requiring similar growing conditions, or plant them later to fill a gap once a vegetable has been harvested. Nasturtiums have large seeds that you can push 1 cm (½ in) down into the compost when planting hanging baskets and window boxes.

Care

Annual flowers growing alongside lettuces, herbs and vegetables in containers need little extra care. Remove any diseased

leaves, and remove faded flowers promptly so more will produce.

Harvesting

Pick the flowers early in the morning, once the dew has dried. There is no need to wash them, but check for insects inside. Place the stems in a jar of cold water, or put the flowers in a plastic bag and store in the refrigerator.

From pastel roses, cheerful violas, bright nasturtiums to dainty borage, pot marigold and fragrant lavender (left to right), there's plenty to choose from when growing edible flowers. The centre of a flower can be bitter, so use only the petals.

A selection of annual flowers

Not all flowers are edible, but the following flowers are safe to eat. (For roses and lavender, see page 50.) Because flowers can share the same common name, even if they are of different species, use the botanical names given below when purchasing seeds.

Nasturtiums *(Tropaeolum majus)* These have a distinct peppery taste, and there are lots of different varieties to choose from, ranging from orange and red to cream flowers; some are trailing plants, while others are bushy. Nasturtiums are easy to grow in hot, dry sites, but they can be a magnet for pests.

Calendula The original pot marigold *(Calendula officinalis)* was bright orange, but there are now variations such as apricot shades, mahogany red and double flowers. The petals have a slight nutty taste; chopped petals add a golden colour to rice or butter.

Violas and violets All violas are edible and have small pretty flowers that tolerate shade. The sweet violets *(Viola odorata)* have the best flavour; this is a hardy perennial plant.

Borage The blue petals of *Borago officinalis* have a cucumber flavour and look pretty floating in summer drinks or added to ice cubes. The plant tolerates some shade and dry conditions.

Garlic

You may never need to buy garlic again if you grow your own, because cloves divide and produce more and more bulbs. Garlic takes up little space, and is easy to grow and store.

Garlic planted in winter on the shortest day can be harvested in early summer on the longest day.

Getting started

What to plant Certified bulbs
Site Sun in moist but well-drained compost
When Plant in spring or autumn to winter
Container size 30 cm (12 in) in diameter
Spacing 15 cm (6 in) for bulbs (less if growing for only leaves)

For the best results, buy certified garlic bulbs from a garden centre or specialist supplier rather than using garlic from a supermarket. Certified garlic bulbs are produced under controlled conditions so there is less risk of plant viruses, and the suppliers will offer garlic varieties that crop well in the UK.

Garlic is divided into two types. Hardneck (rocambole) types have a twisting central shoot that hardens in late summer with the cloves forming around it. Hardneck varieties do well in cold areas and have a strong flavour, but they do not store well. If you live in a warm area, you can choose softneck varieties, which have a bulb with several layers of overlapping cloves, like an artichoke; these store well.

Planting

Remove the papery skin and separate the bulb into cloves. Plant each one upright, with the flat base of the clove pointing down. Push down so the tops are just covered. Birds pull out the cloves, so protect them with netting until the shoots form.

Care

Once planted, garlic needs little care, but it does not like to be crowded by other plants. Keep the compost moist in dry spells. Plants may run to seed and produce a long flower stalk or 'scape'; there may still be a crop at the base but it will not store as well. You can cut up the scapes and use them to flavour dishes. When the tops of the leaves start to dry off, pull back the compost to expose the bulb so it can cure.

Harvesting

Dry the bulbs in the sun or, if rain is due, move then to dry indoors on a sunny windowsill. Rub any dry compost off the bulbs and store them in a dry and cool but frost-free location – a kitchen is often not the best place because it is too humid.

If you have lots of bulbs (at least nine) with long lengths of dead leaves attached, you can make a garlic plait to hang up for storage. Start with three bulbs, then add three more at a time, braiding the dead leaves as you go. At the end, loop the dead leaves over and tie in place so you can hang up the plait.

Using extra garlic

If you have more garlic cloves than you need for growing garlic, they still serve a purpose. Plant them in small pots of compost, then harvest the green shoots to use as a substitute for chives. You can also plant whole bulbs of garlic to produce a large clump of green shoots.

Marjoram & Oregano

Both marjoram and oregano are Mediterranean plants, often used as a flavouring in dishes from that region. These trouble-free plants produce flowers loved by butterflies and bees.

Getting started

What to plant Plants
Site Warm, sunny, in well-drained compost
When Plant in late spring
Container size Varies, but at least 30 cm (12 in) in diameter
Spacing 15–30 cm (6–12 in) apart

To get the intense flavour from the leaves, these plants need warm, dry conditions. In addition to sweet marjoram *(Origanum majorana)* and oregano *(O. vulgare),* you might also come across pot marjoram *(O. onites),* a low-spreading perennial that is useful for containers. Greek oregano is a type of *O. vulgare* that has a more pungent aroma but is less hardy. If in doubt, rub a leaf between finger and thumb to check the aroma. There are also golden or yellow-leaved forms that look attractive in pots.

Planting

You can plant hardy species in the spring, but first harden them off if they have been indoors. For tender types, wait until after the last frost. To grow perennials, use a loam-based compost with grit to improve drainage.

Care

To encourage bushy growth, pinch out the shoot tips. Oregano is a vigorous perennial; when it is too large for the pot, divide the clump and replant healthy young sections.

Harvesting

Pick leaves as soon as the plant is growing well. Cut the plants back to the base several times during the growing season. They will grow again, so even a single plant will yield enough leaves for drying.

The leaves of oregano are at their peak in the warmer months, which is the best time for harvesting.

Drying herbs in a microwave

The dried leaves of marjoram and oregano have a more intense aroma than fresh leaves. You can hang them up in a well-ventilated place for a week or speed up the pace by using a microwave. Microwave drying works best in small batches – a few handfuls of leaves at a time. Remove any diseased or dead leaves, then wash the herbs in cold water and pat dry between kitchen paper. Scatter the leaves in a single layer over two sheets of kitchen paper and microwave for 2 minutes. They should be brittle but still green; if not, microwave again for 30–60 seconds. Crumble the leaves between finger and thumb and store in a clean airtight jar. Label with the herb name and date and use within six months.

Grow sweet marjoram as an annual herb for its delicate, aromatic leaves. Grow it alone or combine it with another herb such as thyme.

Mint

From sauces to teas, mint is a popular herb in the kitchen. The plants are hardy and easy to grow, but there is a knack to keeping up a regular supply of healthy leaves.

Getting started

What to plant Plants
Site Some sun or partial shade
When Plant in spring
Container size Minimum 35 cm (14 in) in diameter
Spacing Minimum 45 cm (18 in)

Mint comes in a huge array with a wide range of flavours, from spearmint and peppermint to pineapple mint, as well as different leaf textures such as the large, soft leaves of 'Apple Mint' and the crinkly leaves of 'Curly'.

Mint plants are hardy and spread through the soil by vigorous underground stems, so they soon swamp other herbs. Even if you buy a container of mixed herbs, replant mint into its own container as soon as possible. An alternative to a pot is to sink a bottomless bucket into the ground, keeping 5–10 cm (2–4 in) above ground, which reduces the need for watering; you will still need to replace the plant in a few years.

Planting

Plant a small potted plant in the centre of a container and water it well. Mint is often one of the first herbs to be available, so you can plant it in early spring (April).

The secret to successfully growing mint is to remember that it is not a Mediterranean herb; mint thrives in moist compost and partial shade.

Care

During the growing season, the plant will spread to the edge of the pot and start to fill it. If it runs out of moisture or nutrients, the middle of the plant will die and the young shoots at the edges will be starved and prone to disease such as rust or powdery mildew. Keep your mint fresh by using a large pot and keeping the compost moist. Move young runners into pots of fresh compost or feed the plants a balanced all-purpose fertiliser. Dispose of any diseased or old plant debris.

The flowers are pretty and are often visited by bees and butterflies, but the seedlings can be a nuisance, even in a pot. Seedlings do not grow like their parent plant and can take over, so pull up any you see.

Harvesting

Mint is a perennial plant, but the leaves are at their peak for harvesting from early summer to early autumn. First, pinch out 2.5 cm (1 in) of the growing tips for use, which will also help the plant to bush out. Later, harvest regularly. When you want to dry a large quantity (see 'Drying herbs in a microwave', page 149) or make a batch of mint sauce, cut the plants down to the base. For fresh mint in winter, dig up runners in autumn and lay them flat in a pot half-filled with compost. Add a thin layer of compost over them and keep on a windowsill.

Parsley

Both flat-leaf parsley and curly parsley are essential herbs. They are tolerant plants that offer regular handfuls of leaves for use raw as a garnish or cooked in sauces.

Getting started

What to plant Seeds
Site Sun or partial shade, moist compost
When Sow seeds in spring to early summer (March to June); sow batches every three months
Container size 15 cm (6 in) in diameter
Spacing 15 cm (6 in)

Parsley tolerates some shade and is reasonably hardy, so even a small space can supply fresh leaves for most of the year. The plant is actually a biennial, forming leaves the first year, flowering then dying in its second year. In practice, however, it is easiest to grow parsley as an annual.

Curly parsley has a wonderful fluffy texture and an intense green colour that looks great in a mixed planting with bright flowers. Flat-leaf parsley is often recommended by chefs for its flavour and is used in salads.

The advantage of growing either type of parsley in pots instead of in the garden is that late and early pickings are less likely to be splashed with soil, which is hard to clean from the leaves. Alternatively, to help keep the leaves clean, you can opt for a variety with longer stems, such as 'Giant Italian Oscar'; this is a vigorous variety that is a good choice for raised beds. At the other extreme, compact varieties such as 'Laura' suit window boxes.

Planting

For regular quantities, grow parsley from seed. Buy a fresh packet of seeds each year. Sprinkle them on the surface of the compost in the final container (parsley doesn't transplant well) and lightly cover with the mix. Keep at 16°C (60°F) and keep the compost moist until the seeds germinate. You can harvest the seedlings early and add to salads, or thin out the seedlings to 2.5 cm (1 in) apart and grow them as larger plants.

Care

Keep the compost moist and watch out for slugs and carrot fly; if the latter attacks the roots, the foliage will turn reddish. Parsley likes partial shade in summer. In warm

The leaves of flat-leaf parsley look similar to those of coriander, but they taste like those of curly parsley.

climates, outdoor sowings do well in winter; a crop cover improves the leaf quality. In cold climates, move the pot indoors to a sunny windowsill.

Harvesting

Cut the plants with a pair of scissors as needed. The stems add plenty of flavour to stocks; however, they are tough to eat raw, so for salads only snip off the leaves. Surplus parsley freezes well. You can either chop the leaves and freeze in ice-cube trays with a little water, or cut the stems and leaves and freeze whole in plastic bags.

Rosemary

An aromatic, evergreen shrub that produces needle-like leaves and attractive small flowers, rosemary is a plant that is more suitable for growing in containers in areas with wet soils.

Getting started

What to plant Plants
Site Sun and shelter in a well-drained compost
When Spring or summer
Container size Minimum 20 cm (8 in) in diameter
Spacing Minimum 20 cm (8 in)

If you keep a young rosemary plant clipped to keep it within bounds, you can partner it with a flowering plant – but make sure its partner tolerates dry soil.

Originally a Mediterranean shrub, rosemary has long been cultivated in Europe and North America as a garden plant. It offers white or pale lavender-blue flowers in late spring. Plants can die in winter because they dislike cold, wet soils. However, in the right conditions, such as a container with plenty of drainage and a loam-based compost plus a couple of handfuls of grit, it can survive in warm areas.

For containers, a young bushy plant or a prostrate form that is less than 15 cm (6 in) high but grows sideways like a mat are two budget options. You can grow a prostrate rosemary in a hanging basket and move it into a conservatory over winter. More stylish, perhaps, is to train a rosemary on a long stem as a mini-standard, with the leaves growing above a main stem. If you grow rosemary in this way, plant different herbs underneath for an attractive planting to display by a front door. There are named

varieties available, such as 'Miss Jessopp's Upright', which is tall but not spreading, and 'Severn Sea', which has light blue flowers and makes a 90 cm (3 ft) mound of arching stems.

Planting

Start with a healthy potted plant in spring and plant it into its final container. Keep the plant watered until it is growing well, then ease off so the compost is barely damp.

Care

Clip the plant after flowering to shape it or let it sprawl. Pinch out the tips to encourage bushy growth. In most regions, rosemary will survive the winter if the compost is well-drained and the roots don't freeze. In case the plant doesn't last, you can take a few 10 cm (4 in) cuttings in summer and plant in damp compost.

Harvesting

Rosemary has a strong flavour, so only small quantities of needles are needed. Start picking needles as soon as the plant is growing well. Use sprigs whole when roasting meat and remove them before serving, or strip the needles from the stems and finely chop to add to dishes. Once the stems harden, you can cut long lengths, strip them of their needles except for the tips, and use as kebab sticks.

Sage

The leaves of this attractive Mediterranean shrub have a strong, pungent aroma, so one or two small, young sage plants should supply you with enough leaves for the kitchen.

The textured leaves of sage make it an attractive plant, especially the varieties with variegated colours, such as this young plant of 'Tricolor'.

Getting started

What to plant Plants
Site Warm, sunny, and well-drained compost
When Plant in spring or summer
Container size 20 cm (8 in) in diameter
Spacing 30 cm (12 in)

Because sage plants have attractive, long-lasting foliage, they work well in mixed plantings. The common sage *(Salvia officinalis)* is a woody plant with plain green leaves, and these leaves are the traditional ones used in cooking. Sage does not like heavy soils, so container planting is a good choice in areas with heavy, clay soils.

Other culinary sages

The salvia family offers other sage plants that have culinary uses. Use clary *(Salvia sclarea)*, a biennial with heart-shaped leaves, like common sage. Or for something different, try the tender pineapple sage *(S. elegans* or *S. rutilans)*, with aromatic leaves that smell like pineapple. Spanish sage *(S. lavandulifolia)* is a hardy sage with narrow leaves. It is highly aromatic compared to more ornamental types.

There are varieties with colourful foliage that are more ornamental plants for containers, and these have enough aroma in the leaves to be good substitutes for common sage. There are three varieties that particularly earn their keep in the garden. 'Icterina', with yellow and green variegated foliage, looks cheerful when paired with yellow flowers or planted in light blue or black containers. 'Tricolor' has green and cream variegated leaves flecked with pink that works beautifully when teamed with pink, whether you choose pink flowers or pink pots. 'Purpuracens', with its brooding, dark purple leaves, provides the perfect foil for pink roses or silver containers.

Planting

You can either buy young sage plants in 7.5 cm (3 in) pots or take 15 cm (6 in) cuttings from already existing sage plants – your own or from a neighbour or friend. If you want to keep the plants for a few years before they get too woody, plant them in a loam-based compost.

Care

Aftercare is minimal; sage is drought tolerant and needs no fertilising.

Harvesting

Sage has a strong flavour, so use it sparingly, picking only a few leaves as required. The foliage will die back in winter, except for in warm climates, so pick and preserve batches of leaves in the summer.

To make sage butter, chop fresh sage and mix it with butter before freezing for up to two months. Dry sage by spreading out the leaves in a single layer to dry in the sun, or use a microwave (see 'Drying herbs in a microwave', page 149). Crumble the dried leaves into airtight jars for storing.

Tarragon

Just a few leaves will add a delicate but warm aniseed flavour to chicken and fish dishes, so it is well worth adding a tarragon plant to your herb collection.

Winter tarragon

You may come across Mexican tarragon (*Tagetes lucida*), also known as sweet-scented marigold, although it rarely flowers in the UK. Grow it as an annual, sowing seeds indoors two months before the last spring frost. Harden off the seedlings before moving it outdoors. The leaves have an aniseed flavour but can also be an irritant.

You can grow tarragon on its own, but it is also the perfect partner for other perennial herbs that prefer dry soil such as winter savory or thyme.

Getting started

What to plant Plants
Site Warm, sun and in well-drained compost
When Plant in late spring to early summer
Container size Minimum 30 cm (12 in) in diameter
Spacing 30 cm (12 in)

Tarragon is an unobtrusive, hardy perennial, with a clump of narrow leaves that rarely flowers. It does best in cool summers; however, it is easy to lose it during winter in cold, wet soils, so it is a good choice for growing in containers, where it does well.

When buying tarragon to use in the kitchen, choose French tarragon (*Artemisia dracunculus* var. *sativa*). Its long, thin leaves have the best flavour. To make sure you are not buying Russian tarragon (*A. dracunculus* ssp. *dracunculoides*), taste a leaf before buying a plant; the leaves of Russian tarragon have a more bitter taste.

Planting

Wait until late spring to early summer before buying a plant, then choose one with some new growth you can taste. Plant into a pot filled with a loam-based compost with some grit, and put it in a warm, sunny spot. Pair it with ornamentals but nothing vigorous because it easily gets swamped.

Care

Water the compost until the plant grows well, then it is tolerant to drought. The plant's growth may slow down, and then start again in autumn. When the top growth dies down, cut away the debris and protect the plant's crown with a mulch such as bark chips. Move the pot indoors in winter or insulate the pot with a double layer of bubble wrap. Buy a new plant every few years.

Harvesting

The harvest period is short (midsummer to early autumn), so pinch out growing tips for kitchen use as soon as the plant is growing. Freeze any surplus or add a sprig to a bottle of vinegar and use in salad dressings.

Thyme

A low-growing, pretty herb with aromatic leaves, thyme thrives in all types of containers, from hanging baskets to shallow pans to pots.

Getting started

What to plant Plants
Site Sun, in a well-drained compost
When Plant in spring
Container size 15 cm (6 in) in diameter
Spacing 20 cm (8 in), but varies, depending on the variety

All thyme plants are woody subshrubs with pungent evergreen leaves that are available most of the year for cooking. To get the most out of these plants, grow thyme plants in containers to keep the leaves clean of mud and debris and put them near the kitchen door.

New plants from old

To propagate, or grow new plants from old ones, divide a large clump in spring or autumn, and then replant the youngest, healthiest sections in fresh compost. Or take 5–8 cm (2–3 in) cuttings from a plant in spring or early summer and plant in a cutting compost or one that drains well. Take cuttings every three to four years to rejuvenate plants.

There is a huge range of thyme plants, and it is fun to have a collection for a variety of flavours to use in the kitchen. The best known for cooking is common thyme (*Thymus vulgaris*), which forms an upright bush with mauve-pink flowers in summer. Those with variegated leaves add interest, either splashed with golden yellow or silver-grey ('Silver Posie'), whereas others such as *T. × citriodorus* have a lemon flavour. In general, the flowers are pretty pink, white or lilac and are loved by bees.

Planting

Thyme is one of the few plants that thrives in shallow baskets or wall planters, but it does like a well-drained compost. A group of thyme plants works well together but, if growing them with other plants, make sure it is not overtaken by its partners and that the compost is not too wet.

Care

Water the plants when young, but thereafter just keep the compost on the dry side. Trim

Thyme plants are small and take up little space, so it is easy to have just a single pot of thyme for a fresh supply of leaves.

plants after flowering to improve their shape and remove any dead stems. You can take cuttings every three or four years to rejuvenate a plant if it starts to get straggly or bare in the centre.

Harvesting

Cut the stems as needed with scissors or secateurs. The leaves pick up dust, so wash the stems, then pick the tiny leaves off in the kitchen. You can use the leaves fresh all winter. Or harvest and dry surplus leaves in summer before the plants flower. Dry in a microwave (see 'Drying herbs in a microwave', page 149).

Strawberries

The aroma and taste of fresh, home-grown strawberries is far superior to any shop-bought offerings, and using containers simplifies the growing of this quick-growing fruit.

Getting started

What to plant Certified virus-free plants
Site Full sun, compost
When Buy potted plants in spring or use rooted runners in early autumn
Container size Minimum 30 cm (12 in) in diameter
Spacing Plant 12.5–15 cm (5–6 in) apart

There are some advantages to growing strawberries in containers instead of in the ground. First, there is no need to keep moving the strawberry bed around the garden every three years to prevent a build-up of soil-borne diseases. The berries are held off the ground so they are cleaner, and you can grow the strawberries in a raised location, which makes them easier to pick without bending down.

Strawberry plants will last three years if you use a durable container full of a loam-based compost and if you can protect the containers over winter in cold areas.

Strawberry plants in raised beds need less watering than those in containers and they are easier to cover with netting, but you will need to create a new bed elsewhere after three years.

Otherwise, grow the plants for only one year, in which case any compost will do.

There are June-bearing varieties that will provide a glut of fruit, as well as everbearing varieties that produce fewer strawberries but over a longer season. Growing three to five of each in their own container will spread the cropping season; however, you have room for only one variety, make it an early June-bearing strawberry.

Another benefit of growing strawberries in lightweight pots is that you can extend their growing season. The trick is to move the pots under cover into a polytunnel or greenhouse over winter, where they will flower up to three weeks earlier than those growing outside. So even if you grow only one variety, having a couple of pots means you can encourage one to fruit earlier than the other.

Planting

After a few years, strawberry plants tend to become infected with plant viruses, so rather than accepting free runners from a neighbour or friend, it is best to order guaranteed virus-free plants from a reliable garden fruit supplier.

On arrival, the plants will look dry and dormant, but they will quickly revive after the roots are well watered, and will grow rapidly. Immediately plant the strawberries into individual pots, insulate the pots over winter, then replant the best into their final pot in spring. The top of the plant's crown should be just above soil level.

Container options

Flowerpots The basic terracotta flowerpot works well if you have room for five or six, along a wall or up steps, for example. Allow for one plant per 15 cm (6 in) diameter pot. With smaller pots, you can move them more easily; for example, to bring them undercover in a greenhouse or conservatory instead of covering with netting when the berries are ripe.

Hanging basket A 30 cm (12 in) diameter hanging basket will hold three strawberry plants with room to sink in an empty plant pot to help direct water into the compost. They will need to be netted against birds, but the netting can be easily attached to the wall bracket.

Planting bags Woven plastic strawberry bags are similar to potato bags but have planting pockets. They are inexpensive and safe for children to use because they can drag them around using the handles. Being a flexible material, the compost tends to separate from the bag, so it needs to be firmed in before watering or the water will run down the inside wall.

Strawberry pot Designed to hold about 12 plants in planting pockets around the sides of the pot as well as at the top, these are difficult to plant and water and can be heavy, but they save on space.

Care

During the first watering, apply it gently, using a rose attachment on the watering can to break up the water into drops. Firm in the compost and adjust the planting, if necessary. Keep the compost moist but not waterlogged and apply a tomato fertiliser as the fruit forms. To prevent birds pecking them, when the fruit starts to swell, cover the pot with netting, making sure it sits away from the strawberries.

If strawberries are planted on all sides of the container, rotate the pot to encourage even growth and ripening. Slugs and snails will eat the fruit; if they can reach a container, apply a copper band around the flowerpots (see pages 110–111).

To maintain the strength of the original strawberry plants, remove runners from the parent plants – this keeps the planting neater, too. Cut off the unhealthy-looking leaves from the parent plant to reduce the

Strawberry plants are short, although the fruit stems can be long, so hanging baskets, as well as tall pots, are suitable containers for growing them.

risk of disease. Replace the plants and compost after two to three years, or sooner if the foliage has yellow streaks and mottling.

Harvesting

You can pick the fruit in the first summer after planting, but the yields can be more than double in the second year. Pick ripe fruit every day or two; strawberries quickly spoil. Pick with the green stem intact, wash the fruit gently and then remove the stem.

Index

Acknowledgements

The author and Toucan Books would like to thank the following people and organisations for their assistance in the preparation of this book:

Steve and Pam Barnett; Nick Hamilton and staff at Barnsdale Gardens; Burgon & Ball; Neil and Tracey Donnelly; Harrod Horticultural; Neil Miller at Hever Castle; Brian Knight at Knights Garden Centre, Nags Hall, Surrey; Tracy Collacott at Mr Fothergill's; Eduardo and Gary at StART SPACE, www. startspace.co.uk; Tom Sharples and Francijn Suermondt at Suttons Seeds; Colin Randel at Thompson & Morgan; Charles Tory; Patrick and Sue Tory; Jim Juby at Vegetalis; and Steve Mercer at *Which? Gardening*.

Photo Credits

Abbreviations: T = Top; M = Middle; B = Bottom; L = Left; R = Right

Front Cover: GAP: Graham Strong (TL); Friedrich Strauss (BL). Photolibrary: Gary K. Smith (TR). Mark Winwood: (ML).

Back Cover: Mark Winwood.

Alamy: 141 Libby Welch (BR).

Ian Armitage: 19 (BR); 81 (TL), (BL), (R); 119 (TR); 120; 125 (BL).

T.C. Bird: 7 (T); 17; 20; 21; 23 (TR); 71; 114; 122; 138–139; 142; 143 (BL); 144; 156.

Jane Courtier: 107; 127.

GAP Photos: Friedrich Strauss 10–11, 12, 13, 83, 105; Gary Smith 14 (BL), 97–98; Victoria Firmston 15; Elke Borkowski 16, 18 (TR), 106; Mark Bolton 22; Graham Strong 23 (BL); Lynn Keddie 27, 85; Lee Avison 112–13; Maxine Adcock 121 (BL), 148; Elke Borkowski 124; Graham Strong 140 (BL); Michael Howes 141 (BL); Claire Davis 141 (BM).

GWI: L. Cole 133.

Getty Images: Heinrich van den Berg 101.

Harrod Horticultural: 19 (TL). **istockphoto:** 135.

LDI: David Murray 75; Sharon Pearson 110; David Murray 111; 126, 136, 137.

Photolibrary: Friedrich Strauss 5; David Cavagnaro 14 (TR); Francesca Yorke 100; Friedrich Strauss 157.

Denis Ryan: 121 (TR).

Shutterstock: valda 102; Nic Neish 103, 119 (BL); macka 130 (BL); Anne Kitzman 130 (BR); Norman Chan 131 (BL), (BM); Artography 130 (TR); Melinda Fawver 138; Yurok 139; 143 (TR), 145 (BL); marykai 145 (TR); Tatiana Markotra 146 (BL) ; Shutterstock 147 (BL), (BM), 151; Calek 155.

Mark Winwood: 2; 6; 7 (M), (B); 8–9; 24–25; 29; 31 (L), (TR), (BR); 33 (L), (TR), (BR); 35; 37; 39 (L), (TR), (BR); 41; 43; 45 (L), (TR), (BR); 47; 48–49; 51 (L), (TR), (BR); 53 (L), (TR), (BR); 55; 57; 59; 61; 63; 65; 67; 69 (L), (TR), (BR); 73 (L), (TR), (BR); 76–77; 79; 87 (RL), (BL), (R); 89; 91; 93; 95 (L), (TR), (BR); 108; 109 (BL), (BM), (BR); 115; 116; 117; 118; 120; 125 (TR); 128 (BL); 129; 131 (BR); 132; 134; 146 (BM); 147 (BR); 149 (BL), (TR); 150; 152; 153; 154.

VegTrug.com: 18 (BL).